KETO MEDITERRANEAN DIET COOKBOOK

103 LOW-CARB EASY AND TASTY RECIPES TO HELP YOU LOSE WEIGHT AND STAY HEALTHY. INCLUDING A 14-DAY MEAL PLAN

Table of Contents

Introduction

Over the past ten years, numerous health researchers have forces doctors and dieticians to change the notion of a healthy diet. As a result, new discoveries have been made that tells more about the true causes and mechanisms of harmful ailments like cancer, diabetes and coronary diseases and for this reason, the previous concept for healthy food has been disregard. Recent research has provided evidence of the benefits of healthy fats in the diet, and this led to the development of the Ketogenic diet. The ketogenic diet is a low-carb and high-fat diet that has become a cornerstone for quick loss of weight. As a result, the Ketogenic diet is associated with improved blood pressure, blood glucose, and insulin levels.

There is another diet that has become a widely accepted nutritional regime, the Mediterranean diet. Mediterranean diet is known for the prevention of coronary diseases and longevity of life. When the concept for a high-fat Ketogenic diet is combined with nutrient density and lifestyle factors of the traditional Mediterranean diet, a new diet comes into the light—the Ketogenic Mediterranean diet.

Ketogenic Mediterranean diet features food that contains 7 to 10 percent carbohydrates, 55 to 65 percent fats, 25 to 30 percent proteins, and 5 to 10 percent alcohol. It is very easy to merge the Mediterranean diet with the Ketogenic diet. Both diets promote eating whole-foods including fresh non-starchy vegetables and fruits, proteins from fish along with eggs, cheese, poultry and meat, high amounts of healthy oils, moderate intake of red wine, and avoiding foods that are processed or contain sugars, chemicals, or additives. The only difference in this diet is slight emphasize on different sources of fats and allowing red wine.

In the following chapters of this eBook, you will find more information about what the Ketogenic diet and the Mediterranean diet is and how their pair is excellent for you.

Chapter 1. The Basics of Mediterranean Diet

What Is the Mediterranean Diet?

Mediterranean diet is a name for food ingredients and recipes involving them used in countries around the Mediterranean Sea, such as Croatia and Greece. As different tribes fluctuated into the area, they brought their own recipes and ideas for preparing the food they found: fish, poultry, olives, wheat, fresh fruits, cheese, grapes, and yogurt. The local populace voted on the recipes by passing them on, which over centuries resulted in the Mediterranean diet. The diet itself has been protected by UNESCO as a cultural heritage. It traditionally uses no eggs, no red meat and just a dash of alcohol, which could explain many health benefits it delivers, such as the lowered risk of heart disease.

Benefits of the Mediterranean Diet

It appears the Mediterranean diet protects against type 2 diabetes, heart disease, weight gain and ballooning waist, most notably due to the presence of unsaturated fats from fish and olive oil, lack of processed foods, and use of spices instead of salt. Type 2 diabetes is a wicked disease caused by a conglomerate of factors, most of which have to do with diet, almost exclusively affecting Western countries. A type 2 diabetic will generally be overweight with a high risk of heart disease, an increased waist circumference and a sedentary lifestyle involving processed sugars, too much salt, and saturated fat from red meat. Lifestyle choices and exposure to the sun at that latitude add to the Mediterranean diet health benefits as well, supplying the person with fresh air, physical activity, and vitamin D.

Why is a Mediterranean Diet Good for You?

A healthy diet is all about making wise choices on a daily basis. Mediterranean diet consists of countless lifetimes of wise choices made by people who wanted to live a long, active and productive life and chose a diet to help them stay fit well into old age. The biggest issues for people in advanced age are chronic weakness, weight gain and lack of mobility, resulting in reliance on their family to remain active. This causes a tremendous amount of stress and anxiety for everyone involved but it doesn't have to be that old people are necessarily quaking and feeble; there's no reason a person can't remain fit and active if fed a proper, nourishing Mediterranean diet.

What Makes a Mediterranean Diet and Lifestyle?

Unsaturated fats from olive oil and omega-3 fatty acids from fish are two key dietary ingredients in the Mediterranean diet; sunshine and vitamin D are two key ingredients for the Mediterranean lifestyle. Medicine is still researching why unsaturated fats and omega-3 fatty acids are healthy for the heart but it appears the two lower the amount of bad cholesterol, LDL, and protect arteries from inflammation that leads to atherosclerosis. Heart disease is extremely complex but the root cause seems to be an unbalanced diet poor in healthy fats, such as that gotten from vegetables and fish. Sunshine stimulates circulation and lifts up the mood while vitamin D serves as a protection for the heart and the immune system. These four things—unsaturated fats, omega-3 fatty acids, sunshine, and vitamin D—appear to be the healthiest combo for longevity, fitness, and good mood.

Keto Diet and Mediterranean Diet

The definition of the 'ideal' diet keeps changing as more research is carried out. Low-fat diets were formerly trendy until it was discovered that it was not beneficial to health or weight loss. We now know that fat is good.

This article would be comparing the differences and similarities between the ketogenic diet and the Mediterranean diet,

The Ketogenic Diet

Initially created in 1920 as a form of therapy for epileptic children, the ketogenic diet which is a low-carb diet has been popularly used since then.

It is high fat (70-80%), moderate protein (15-20%), and a low carb diet. The ketogenic diet aims to drive the body into a ketotic state where all the body's carb reservoir is depleted. Ketosis is beneficial to health and might help to prevent some chronic diseases.

Ketogenic foods are:

1. Animal protein such as fish, beef, eggs, poultry, and organ meat.
2. Low-carb vegetables with no starch.
3. Zero sugar, flour, or refined food.
4. Little or no fruits. Only fruit with low sugar content like berries is permitted.
5. Fats in the form of butter, nut, healthy oils, and avocado.

Mediterranean Diet

The popular Mediterranean diet is based on the lifestyle of people in the Mediterranean countries (Spain, France, Italy) between 1940 and 1950. Although there is a slight variation in the actual diet. According to research, the menu is made up of 50% carbs, 30% fats, and 29% protein. Mediterranean foods include:

1. Beans and legumes like lentils and peas.
2. Rich fruits and vegetables.
3. Whole grains like quinoa, brown rice.
4. Reduced amount of meat products.
5. Little or no processed foods, flour, or sugar.
6. Moderate wine drinking.
7. A dairy product such as cheese and yogurt.
8. Fish as the primary source of protein for non-vegetarians

After it was discovered that this diet reduces the risk of chronic diseases including heart diseases, this diet became a favorable recommendation. These benefits are attributed to the oleic acid contained in olive oil and polyphenols in red wine.

Similarities between the Ketogenic Diet and Mediterranean Diet

1. Sodium Consumption

They both promote sodium intake. Mediterranean diet is rich in salt as a result of the oily dressings with increased amounts of salt and foods like cheese, olives, and anchovies. The Keto diet encourages the addition of salts to maintain electrolytes balance since the meals are low in salt.

2. Healthy food

They both promote the consumption of protein and fresh vegetables and do not permit the use of chemicals, sugars, processed foods, or additives.

3. Health benefits

There are many health benefits. Keto diet reduces the levels of total and LDL cholesterol, reduces the levels of triglycerides and increases the levels of HDL cholesterol which could be beneficial for people with type 2 diabetes and in fighting some cancers. Mediterranean diet advocates the use of olive oil which has been discovered to reduce the risk of heart disease, death, and stroke.

Differences between the Ketogenic and Mediterranean Diet

Fat Consumption

Mediterranean diet has a lower fat percentage than the ketogenic diet. Mediterranean diet also advocates the use of unsaturated like gotten from fish and oils whereas keto foods include both saturated and unsaturated oils.

Carbohydrate Consumption

The Mediterranean diet advocates high carb, healthy fats, and no refined sugars whereas the ketogenic diet restricts carbs in every form.

Conclusion

They are both beneficial to health. It is advisable to start with the Mediterranean diet before moving to the ketogenic diet.

Ketogenic Mediterranean Diet

The Ketogenic Mediterranean diet involves 5-10% of alcohol, 7-10% of carbohydrates, 55-65% of fat, and 22-30% of protein.
Foods include:

1. Non-starchy vegetables and plenty of salads.
2. Plenty of healthy oils such as olive oil
3. Moderate wine drinking
4. Major protein source from fatty fish, lean meat, cheese, and eggs

Similar to the ketogenic diet, there is a total restriction of sugars, flours, and starch. The only difference is that the fat source is different from the ketogenic diet and red wine is permitted.

The Mediterranean Ketogenic Diet

Ever wondered what diet plan would be created from blending the mysterious Mediterranean diet with a structured ketogenic diet? This is where the Mediterranean ketogenic diet comes in. The critical components of this diet include olive oil, red wine, fish, and salad.
A few of the critical points of a structure ketogenic diet are:

1. Main protein source was fish.
2. Every day, the subject was asked to drink moderate amounts of wine.
3. Carbs were gotten mainly from salads and green vegetables.
4. Unrestricted calories. Eating foods rich in fats creates a feeling of satiety, and this helps to suppress hunger.

Research Subjects of the Mediterranean Ketogenic Diets

This 12-week study was conducted with 40 obese subjects with an average Body Mass Index of 37; it was based on replacing their regular diet that promotes diabetes with a diet 50% rich in carbohydrates. The research was successful.
Ketone blood strips were used to confirm ketone levels each morning. I am afraid I have to disagree with this because if ketone urine strips were used instead, the result would be incorrect after 2 or 3 weeks.
Results of this study include:

1. These subjects had their weight reduced to 208 pounds, from an initial 240 pounds.
2. Evident fat loss in place of muscle loss
3. Reduction in blood pressure
4. Improvement in blood lipids.
5. Increase in HDL cholesterol
6. Reduction in blood glucose levels by about 29mg/dl
7. Reduction in levels of triglycerides which in turn reduces the risks of cancer, stroke, and heart disease.

Six Key Principles of the Mediterranean Ketogenic Diet

1. For many times, skip meals, eat heavy meals followed by periods of no meals

Although heavy meals provide the nutrients that are essential for maximum functioning while also ensuring that our weight is healthy, it is not advisable to eat them throughout the day. Try not to snack. In actual Mediterranean diets, the Greeks are known to fast for about three months, this is responsible for the benefits of enhanced mental function, and improved heart function.

2. Green, leafy vegetables

It is essential to include green leafy vegetables or cruciferous vegetables in each meal. They contain chemicals that improve immunity and fight cancer. Although the amount to be consumed depends on each person.

3. Instead of sweet foods, eat bitter foods

Similar to cruciferous and green vegetables, bitter foods like onions, bitter vegetables, bitter red wine, herbs, and garlic are rich in chemicals that improve the body's immunity. They prevent your taste buds from getting addicted to sweet and potentially unhealthy foods. Bitter foods also aid detoxification.

4. Minimize the quantity

Most effective diets involve some form of carbohydrate restriction to lower blood glucose and suppress insulin while helping the body eliminate toxins. Although there is no standard value, nutritional ketosis needs less than 20 to 25grams each day while a very low or low carb diet is between 0 to 150grams each day. Sources of carbohydrates can include sweet potato, blackberries, and yucca. They are usually optimized faster after exercising.

5.   Consume large amounts of fat

A strict intermittent ketogenic diet is based on ample quantities of fat. The monounsaturated oil used in the Mediterranean diet is a good idea. Use rich cream, palm oil, macadamia, avocado and coconut oil with particularly for dressing, and with moderation.

6.   Engage in routine exercises

Engage in periods of exercises including resistance training and heavy weight lifting. It is important to know that the people of the Mediterranean engage in important routine exercise. They frequently take walks, engage in heavy lifting. Muscle contraction produces chemical substances that fight against cancer and inflammation.

Rs: Relaxation, Recovery and Rest

In a society that is always on the go, we restrict the definition is a healthy lifestyle to only good and productivity.
We still require enough rest in various firms like sleep that enhances metabolism, regulate levels of blood glucose and boost immunity. You can engage your mind and also relax by socializing and reading. Other activities like gardening might require the use of your mind.
The mind, just like the body, needs to be rejuvenated.
These seven fundamental principles have been beneficial to me in maintaining a healthy lifestyle and weight. It has also helped to nourish my mind and body.
While on vacation recently, a few intense physical activities showed how I have unconsciously followed these principles. I recall my grandfather following similar principles. Although, part of his diet might not align with the principles of a Mediterranean ketogenic lifestyle there are quite some similarities.

Chapter 2. About the Fats: Extra Virgin Olive Oil

Reasons to Prove That Extra Virgin Olive Oil is The Healthiest Oil in Existence

Many controversies are surrounding the inclusion of fat in the diet. It is common for people to argue about seed oils, animal fats, and almost any type of fat.

However, out of all these fats, extra virgin olive oil is one fat that many people seem to agree on.

A staple in the Mediterranean diet, olive oil is a traditional fat that has been regularly included in the diets of some of the healthiest populations in the world.

Also, some studies have been conducted on the benefits of olive oil on health.

The researchers discovered that the antioxidants and fatty acids contained in olive oil are responsible for their significant benefits on the health, like lowering the risk of heart disease.

Olive Oil – Definition and Production Processes

Olive oil is extracted from olives, the fruit produced by olive trees. The procedure is a straightforward one, the olives are pressed, and the olive starts to drop.

Although there is a significant issue with olive oil, its appearance can be deceptive. Poor quality olive oils can be gotten with the use of chemicals or even mixing with other less expensive oils.

It is essential to buy authentic olive oil.

The most authentic type is the extra virgin olive oil. It is processed naturally and checked for impurities and some sensory properties like smell and taste.

Genuine extra virgin olive oil has a peculiar taste and is rich in phenolic antioxidants, and this is the primary ingredient that is responsible for the benefits derived from natural olive oil.

Also, some olive oils are healthy, processed or 'thin,' they are gotten by using solvents, or heat, cheap oils such as canola and soybean oils have been used to dilute some of them.

This is the reason why extra virgin olive oil is the only type I would suggest.

Nutrient Contained in Extra Virgin Olive Oil

Extra virgin olive oil is moderately nourishing.

Moderate quantities of Vitamin K and E and a lot of critical fatty acids are contained in olive oil.

The nutritional composition of 100g of olive oil is:

- Vitamin E: 75% of RDA
- Omega-3: 0.76% of RDA
- Vitamin K: 75% of RDA
- Saturated fat: 13.8% of RDA
- Omega-6: 9.7% of RDA
- Monounsaturated fat: 73% of RDA (almost entirely oleic acid)

However, the primary benefit of extra virgin olive oil is in the composition of antioxidants.

Antioxidants are organic compounds that help prevent diseases.

The vital antioxidants it contains includes oleuropein which prevents the oxidation of LDL Cholesterol and oleocanthal which is a potent anti-inflammatory compound.

Anti-Inflammatory compounds are contained in Extra Virgin Olive Oil. It is a widespread belief that most diseases are due to chronic inflammation; including cancer, diabetes, arthritis, metabolic syndromes, Alzheimer's, and heart disease.

Some hypothesis suggests that the anti-inflammatory properties of olive oil are responsible for the majority of its benefits.

Evidence suggests that the primary fatty acid contained in olive oil- oleic acid can help to lower inflammatory substances like C-Reactive Protein. Although, the significant anti-inflammatory properties are due to the antioxidants contained in olive oil, especially oleocanthal which has been discovered to produce effects similar to ibuprofen, a widely used anti-inflammatory drug.

Various studies have estimated that the quantity of oleocanthal in 3 to 4 tablespoons (around 50mls) of extra virgin olive oil works in the same way as 10% of the dosage of ibuprofen in an adult to relieve pain. Another research also discovered that compound present in olive oil could suppress the proteins and genes that promote inflammation. Remember that chronic, low-level inflammation usually is mild and the damage is done after many years or decades.

Extra Virgin Olive Oil Protects Against Diseases of the Cardiovascular System

Diseases of the cardiovascular system such as stroke or heart disease are the most popular causes of death worldwide.
Many researchers have discovered that death resulting from these diseases is low in specific areas such as the countries at the border of the Mediterranean Sea.
This research made people curious about the Mediterranean Diet, that is presumed to imitate the eating habits of people in those countries.
Researches on the Mediterranean diet have discovered that it can help to fight against heart disease. According to one significant study, it lowered strokes, death, and heart attacks by 30%.
These are some of the mechanisms with which Extra Virgin olive oil prevents heart diseases.

- Reduces inflammation: As stated previously, olive oil is anti-inflammatory; inflammation is responsible for most heart diseases.
- LDL cholesterol: Olive oil prevents the oxidation of LDL cholesterol which is a significant process in the development of heart disease.
- Enhances the functions of the endothelium: The endothelium is the inner layer of blood vessels; olive oil improves endothelial function.

Other Health Benefits

Though it is mostly studied for the benefits of health, consuming olive oil also has some advantages

Olive Oil and Cancer

One major cause of death is cancer. Cancer is caused by the unlimited growth of the body's cells.

Research has discovered that people in the Mediterranean have a moderately reduced risk of cancer and there have been some theories that suggest that it might be due to olive oil.

The oleic acid present in olive oil prevents oxidation and has been discovered to be beneficial in protecting against cancer-promoting genes. Some in-vitro research has discovered that some substances in olive oil can fight against cancer at the level of molecules.

Although, there have been no human trials to prove that olive oil can prevent cancer.

Olive Oil and Alzheimer's Disease

The most common neurodegenerative disease in the world is Alzheimer's disease, which is also a significant cause of dementia.

Alzheimer's disease is caused by the accumulation of protein products known as beta-amyloid plaques in specific neurons in the brain.

One trial involving humans discovered that a Mediterranean diet rich in olive oil has beneficial effects on the functions of the brain and lowers the risks associated with mental deterioration.

Can It Be Used to Prepare Your Meals?

Cooking can cause the oxidation of fatty acids. This means that they react with oxygen and are destroyed.

This is mainly due to the double bonds in the fatty acid molecules. Because of this, saturated fats (without double bonds) are not easily destroyed by increased temperature; whereas, polyunsaturated fats (a lot of double bonds) are susceptible and are destroyed.

Olive oil, which is rich in monounsaturated fatty acids (just one double bond) is not easily destroyed by high heat.

One research involved heating extra virgin love oil at a temperature of 356 degrees Fahrenheit (180 degrees Celsius) for a period of 36 hours. The olive oil was not destroyed easily.

Another research deep-fried with olive oil and harmful levels were only reached after about 24-27 hours.

To sum this up, olive oil is not harmful even when cooking at moderately high temperatures.

Chapter 3. Breakfast Recipes

1. Greek Style Frittata with Spinach and Feta Cheese

Preparation Time: 10 minutes
Cooking Time: 3.5-4 hours on low
Servings: 6
Ingredients:

- 2 cups spinach, fresh or frozen
- 8 eggs, lightly beaten
- 1 cup plain yogurt
- 1 small onion, cut into small pieces
- 2 red roasted peppers, peeled
- 1garlic clove, crushed
- 1 cup feta cheese, crumbled
- 2 Tablespoons softened butter
- 2 Tablespoons olive oil
- Salt and pepper to taste
- 1 teaspoon dried oregano

Directions:

1. Sauté the onion and garlic for 5 minutes. Add the spinach, heat for an additional 2 minutes. Let the mixture cool down.
2. Roast the red peppers in a dry pan or under the broiler. Peel them and cut them into small pieces. You can use roasted peppers from a jar, but use those without vinegar.
3. In a separate bowl, beat the eggs, yogurt, and seasoning. Combine well.
4. Add the peppers and the onion mixture. Mix again.
5. Crumble the feta cheese with a fork, add it to the frittata.
6. Grease the bottom and sides of the crock-pot with butter. Pour the mixture in.
7. Cover, cook on low for 3.5-4 hours.
8. Serve with avocado slices sprinkled with grated Parmesan.

Nutrition:

- Net C: 9g
- P: 18g
- F: 25g

2. Cheese & Cauliflower Bake

Preparation Time: 5 minutes
Cooking Time: 4 hours on low
Servings: 6
Ingredients:

- 1 head cauliflower, cut into florets
- ½ cup cream cheese
- ¼ cup whipping cream
- 2 Tablespoons lard (or butter, if you prefer)
- 1 Tablespoon lard (or butter, if you prefer) to grease the crock-pot
- 1 teaspoon salt
- ½ teaspoon fresh ground black pepper
- ½ cup yellow cheese, Cheddar, shredded
- 6 slices of bacon, crisped and crumbled

Directions:

1. Grease the crock-pot.
2. Add all the ingredients, except the cheese and the bacon.
3. Cook on low for 3 hours.
4. Open the lid and add cheese. Re-cover, cook for an additional hour.
5. Top with the bacon and serve.

Nutrition:

- Calories: 278
- Fat: 15g

- Net Carbohydrates: 3g
- Protein: 32g
- Fiber: 1g
- Net Carbs: 2g

3. Ham & Cheese Broccoli Brunch Bowl

Preparation Time: 5 minutes
Cooking Time: 8 hours on low
Servings: 6
Ingredients:

- 1 medium head of broccoli, chopped small
- 4 cups vegetable broth
- 2 Tablespoons olive oil
- 1 teaspoon mustard seeds, ground
- 3garlic cloves, minced
- Salt and pepper to taste
- 2 cups Cheddar cheese, shredded
- 2 cups ham, cubed
- Pinch of paprika

Directions:

1. Add all ingredients to the crock-pot in order of the list.
2. Cover, cook on low for 8 hours.

Nutrition:

- Calories: 690
- Fat: 48g
- Carbohydrates: 16g
- Protein: 40g
- Fiber: 3g
- Net Carbohydrates: 13g

4. Zucchini & Spinach with Bacon

Preparation Time: 10 minutes
Cooking Time: 6 hours on low
Servings: 6
Ingredients:

- 8 slices bacon
- 1 Tablespoon olive oil
- 4 medium zucchini, cubed
- 2 cups baby spinach
- 1 red onion, diced
- 6garlic cloves, sliced thin
- 1 cup chicken broth
- Salt and pepper to taste

Directions:

1. In a pan, heat the olive oil, brown the bacon for 5 minutes. Break it into pieces in the pan.
2. Place remaining ingredients in crock-pot, pour the bacon and fat from the pan over the ingredients.
3. Cover, cook on low for 6 hours.

Nutrition:

- Calories: 171
- Fat: 16g
- Net Carbohydrates: 6g
- Protein: 2g
- Fiber: 2g
- Carbohydrates: 8g

5. Pepperoni Pizza with Meat Crust

Preparation Time: 5 minutes
Cooking Time: 4 hours on low
Servings: 6
Ingredients:

- 2.2. pounds lean ground beef
- 2garlic cloves, minced
- 1 Tablespoon dry, fried onions
- Salt and pepper to taste
- 2 cups shredded mozzarella
- 1 ¾ cup sugarless ready-made pizza sauce
- 2 cups shredded yellow cheese, Cheddar
- ½ cup sliced pepperoni

Directions:

1. In a pan, brown the beef with the seasoning together.
2. Mix the beef with the cheese.
3. Butter the crock-pot and spread the crust out evenly over the bottom.
4. Pour the pizza sauce over the crust and spread evenly.
5. Top with the cheese and arrange the pepperoni slices.
6. Cover, cook on low for 4 hours.

Nutrition:

- Calories: 221
- Fat: 9g
- Net Carbohydrates: 8g
- Protein: 21g
- Fiber: 2g
- Carbohydrates: 10g

6. The Better Quiche Lorraine

Preparation Time: 5 minutes
Cooking Time: 4 hours on low
Servings: 8
Ingredients:

- 1 Tablespoon butter
- 10 eggs, beaten
- 1 cup heavy cream
- 1 cup Cheddar cheese, shredded
- Pinch fresh ground black pepper
- 10 strips of bacon, crisped and crumbled
- ½ cup fresh spinach, chopped

Directions:

1. Butter the crock-pot.
2. In a large bowl, mix all the ingredients, except bacon crumbles.
3. Transfer mixture to the crock-pot, sprinkle bacon on top.
4. Cover, cook on low for 4 hours. (In the last 15 minutes' watch carefully, not to overcook it.)

Nutrition:

- Calories: 260
- Fat: 21g
- Net Carbohydrates: 4g
- Protein: 14g
- Fiber: 1g
- Carbohydrates: 5g

7. Spinach & Sausage Pizza

Preparation Time: 5 minutes
Cooking Time: 4-6 hours on low
Servings: 8
Ingredients:

- 1 Tablespoon olive oil
- 1 cup lean ground beef
- 2 cups spicy pork sausage
- 2garlic cloves, minced
- 1 Tablespoon dry, fried onions
- Salt and pepper to taste
- 1 ¾ cups sugarless ready-made pizza sauce
- 3 cups fresh spinach
- ½ cup sliced pepperoni
- ¼ cup pitted black olives, sliced
- ¼ cup sun-dried tomatoes, chopped
- ½ cup spring onions, chopped
- 3 cups shredded mozzarella

Directions:

1. In a pan, heat the olive oil. Brown the beef, then the pork. Drain the oil off both portions of meat, mix together.
2. Pour the meat in the crock-pot. Spread evenly and press down.
3. Alternate in layers: pizza sauce, toppings, and cheese.
4. Cover and cook on low for 4-6 hours.

Nutrition:

- Calories: 259
- Fat: 13g
- Carbohydrates: 5g
- Protein: 16g
- Fiber: 2g
- Net Carbohydrates: 7g

8. Eggplant & Sausage Bake

Preparation Time: 10 minutes
Cooking Time: 4 hours on low
Servings: 6
Ingredients:

- 2 cups eggplant, cubed, salted, and drained
- 1 Tablespoon olive oil
- 2.2 pounds' spicy pork sausage
- 1 Tablespoon Worcestershire sauce
- 1 Tablespoon mustard
- 2 regular cans of Italian diced tomatoes
- 1 jar tomato passata
- 2 cups mozzarella cheese, shredded

Directions:

1. Grease the crock pot with olive oil.
2. Mix the sausage, Worcestershire sauce, and mustard. Pour the mixture into the crock-pot.
3. Top the meat mixture with eggplant.
4. Pour the tomatoes over the mixture, sprinkle with grated cheese.
5. Cover, cook on low for 4 hours.

Nutrition:

- Calories: 467
- Fat: 41g
- Carbohydrates: 3g
- Protein: 20g
- Fiber: 2g
- Net Carbohydrates: 1g

9. Three-Cheese Artichoke Hearts Bake

Preparation Time: 5 minutes
Cooking Time: 2 hours on high
Servings: 6
Ingredients:

- 1 cup Cheddar cheese, grated
- ½ cup dry Parmesan cheese
- 1 cup cream cheese
- 1 cup spinach, chopped
- 1 clove of garlic, crushed
- 1 jar artichoke hearts, chopped
- Salt and pepper to taste

Directions:

1. Place all the ingredients in the crock-pot. Mix lightly.
2. Cover, cook on high for 2 hours.

Nutrition:

- Calories: 141
- Fat: 11.5g
- Carbohydrates: 0.6g
- Protein: 8.9g
- Fiber: 0g
- Net Carbohydrates: 0.5g

10. Tomato Eggs

Preparation Time: 5 minutes
Cooking Time: 5 minutes
Servings: 2
Ingredients:

- 1 tomato, chopped
- 1 teaspoon sunflower oil
- 1 cup fresh parsley, chopped
- 3 eggs, beaten
- 1 oz. Feta cheese, crumbled

Directions:

1. Heat sunflower oil in the pan.
2. Then add chopped tomatoes and parsley—Cook the ingredients for 2 minutes.
3. After this, add eggs and stir the mixture well.
4. Cook the dish for 2 minutes more, add feta cheese, and stir well. Cook the meal for 1 more minute.

Nutrition:

- Calories: 169
- Protein: 11.5g
- Carbohydrates: 4.2g

- Fat: 12.2g
- Fiber: 1.4g
- Cholesterol: 258mg

11. Sun-Dried Tomatoes Salad

Preparation Time: 15 minutes
Cooking Time: 0 minutes
Servings: 4
Ingredients:
- 1 cup sun-dried tomatoes, chopped
- 4 eggs, hard-boiled, peeled, and chopped
- ½ cup olives, pitted, chopped
- 1 small red onion, finely chopped
- ½ cup Greek yogurt
- 1 teaspoon lemon juice
- 1 teaspoon Italian seasonings

Directions:
1. In the salad bowl, mix up all ingredients and shake well.

Nutrition:

- Calories: 120
- Protein: 8.8g
- Carbohydrates: 5.9g
- Fat: 7.1g
- Fiber: 1.5g

12. Greek Bowl

Preparation Time: 10 minutes
Cooking Time: 7 minutes
Servings: 6
Ingredients:
- ¼ cup Greek yogurt

- 12 eggs
- ¼ teaspoon ground black pepper
- ½ teaspoon salt
- 1 tablespoon avocado oil
- 1 cup cherry tomatoes, chopped
- 1 cup quinoa, cooked
- 1 cup fresh cilantro, chopped
- 1 red onion, sliced

Directions:
1. Boil the eggs in the water within 7 minutes. Then cool them in the cold water and peel.
2. Chop the eggs roughly and put them in the salad bowl.
3. Add Greek yogurt, ground black pepper, salt, avocado oil, tomatoes, quinoa, cilantro, and red onion.
4. Shake the mixture well. Serve.

Nutrition:

- Calories: 253
- Protein: 16.2g
- Carbohydrates: 22.4g
- Fat: 11g
- Fiber: 2.9g

13. Morning Oats

Preparation Time: 5 minutes
Cooking Time: 0 minutes
Servings: 2
Ingredients:
- 1 oz. pecans, chopped
- ¼ cup oats
- ½ cup plain yogurt
- 1 date, chopped
- ½ teaspoon vanilla extract

Directions:

1. Mix up all ingredients and leave for 5 minutes.
2. Then transfer the meal to the serving bowls.

Nutrition:

- Calories: 196
- Protein: 6.5g
- Carbohydrates: 16.5g
- Fat: 11.6g
- Fiber: 2.9g

14. Yogurt with Dates

Preparation Time: 10 minutes
Cooking Time: 0 minutes
Servings: 4
Ingredients:
- 5 dates, pitted, chopped
- 2 cups plain yogurt
- ½ teaspoon vanilla extract
- 4 pecans, chopped

Directions:
1. Mix up all ingredients in the blender and blend until smooth.
2. Pour it into the serving cups.

Nutrition:

- Calories: 215
- Protein: 8.7g
- Carbohydrates: 18.5g
- Fat: 11.5g
- Fiber: 2.3g

15. Spinach Frittata

Preparation Time: 15 minutes
Cooking Time: 20 minutes
Servings: 6
Ingredients:
- ¼ cup Kalamata olives, pitted and chopped
- 8 eggs, beaten
- 2 cups spinach, chopped
- 1 tablespoon olive oil
- ½ teaspoon chili flakes
- 2 oz. Feta, crumbled
- ¼ cup plain yogurt

Directions:
1. Brush the pan with olive oil. After this, mix up all remaining ingredients in the mixing bowl, and pour them into the pan.
2. Bake the frittata for 20 minutes at 355°F. Serve.

Nutrition:

- Calories: 145
- Protein: 9.6g
- Carbohydrates: 2.3g
- Fat: 10.9g
- Fiber: 0.4g

16. Baked Eggs with Parsley

Preparation Time: 15 minutes
Cooking Time: 20 minutes
Servings: 6
Ingredients:
- 2green bell peppers, chopped
- 3 tablespoons olive oil
- 1 yellow onion, chopped
- 1 teaspoon sweet paprika

- 6 tomatoes, chopped
- 6 eggs
- ¼ cup parsley, chopped

Directions:
1. Warm a pan with the oil over medium heat, add all ingredients except eggs and roast them for 5 minutes.
2. Stir the vegetables well and crack the eggs.
3. Transfer the pan with eggs in the preheated to 360°F oven and bake them for 15 minutes.

Nutrition:

- Calories: 167
- Protein: .3g
- Carbohydrates: 10.2g
- Fat: 11.8g
- Fiber: 2.6g

17. Mushroom Casserole

Preparation Time: 15 minutes
Cooking Time: 60 minutes
Servings: 4
Ingredients:
- 2 eggs, beaten
- 1 cup mushrooms, sliced
- 2 shallots, chopped
- 1 teaspoon marjoram, dried
- ½ cup artichoke hearts, chopped
- 3 oz. Cheddar cheese, shredded
- ½ cup plain yogurt

Directions:
1. Mix up all ingredients in the casserole mold and cover it with foil.
2. Bake the casserole for 60 minutes at 355°F.

Nutrition:

- Calories: 156

- Protein: 11.2g
- Carbohydrates: 6.2g
- Fat: 9.7g
- Fiber: 1.3g

18. Vanilla Pancakes

Preparation Time: 15 minutes
Cooking Time: 5 minutes
Servings: 2
Ingredients:
- 6 ounces' plain yogurt
- ½ cup whole-grain flour
- 1 egg, beaten
- 1 teaspoon vanilla extract
- 1 teaspoon baking powder

Directions:
1. Heat non-stick skillet well. Meanwhile, mix up all ingredients.
2. Pour the mixture into the skillet in the shape of the pancakes. Cook them for 1 minute per side. Serve.

Nutrition:

- Calories: 202
- Protein: 11.7g
- Carbohydrates: 29.4g
- Fat: 3.8g
- Fiber: 3.7g

19. Savory Egg Galettes

Preparation Time: 15 minutes
Cooking Time: 30 minutes
Servings: 4
Ingredients:

- ¼ cup white onion, diced
- ¼ cup bell pepper, chopped
- ½ teaspoon salt
- 1 teaspoon chili flakes
- 2 tablespoons olive oil
- 1 teaspoon dried dill
- 6 eggs, beaten
- 2 tablespoons plain yogurt

Directions:
1. Mix up onion, bell pepper, salt, and chili flakes in the pan. Add olive oil and dried dill. Sauté the ingredients for 5 minutes.
2. Then pour the beaten eggs into the square baking mold. Add sautéed onion mixture and plain yogurt.
3. Flatten the mixture and bake in the preheated to 360°F oven for 20 minutes. Cut the meal into galettes. Serve.

Nutrition:

- Calories: 166
- Protein: 9g
- Carbohydrates: 2.4g
- Fat: 13.5g
- Fiber: 0.3g

20. Arugula Frittata

Preparation Time: 15 minutes
Cooking Time: 25 minutes
Servings: 12
Ingredients:
- 3garlic cloves, minced
- 1 tablespoon olive oil
- 1 cup fresh arugula, chopped
- 8 eggs, beaten
- 1 teaspoon ground black pepper
- 1 cup mozzarella cheese, shredded

Directions:

1. Warm the olive oil in the pan. Mix up eggs with ground black pepper, arugula, and garlic cloves.
2. Add arugula and pour the mixture into the hot pan. Top the egg mixture with mozzarella and transfer in the preheated to 360°F oven. Bake the frittata for 20 minutes. Serve.

Nutrition:

- Calories: 61
- Protein: 4.5g
- Carbohydrates: 0.7g
- Fat: 4.5g
- Fiber: 0.1g

21. Breakfast Toast

Preparation Time: 10 minutes
Cooking Time: 20 minutes
Servings: 6
Ingredients:

- 2 eggs, beaten
- ½ cup yogurt
- 1 banana, mashed
- ½ teaspoon ground cinnamon
- 6 whole-grain bread slices
- 1 tablespoon olive oil

Directions:

1. In the mixing bowl, mix up eggs, cream, and ground cinnamon, add mashed banana.
2. Coat the bread in the egg mixture. Then heat olive oil.
3. Put the coated bread in the hot olive oil and roast for 3 minutes per side or light brown.

Nutrition:

- Calories: 153
- Protein: 6.2g

- Carbohydrates: 19.2g
- Fat: 5.6g
- Fiber: 2.6g

22. Artichoke Omelet

Preparation Time: 5 minutes
Cooking Time: 10 minutes
Servings: 4
Ingredients:

- 4 eggs, beaten
- 1 tomato, chopped
- ½ cup artichoke hearts, chopped
- 4 oz. goat cheese, crumbled
- 1 tablespoon olive oil

Directions:

1. Mix up eggs, chopped artichokes, goat cheese, and tomato. Then brush the baking mold with olive oil and pour the mixture inside.
2. Bake the omelet for 10 minutes at 365°F. Serve.

Nutrition:

- Calories: 231
- Protein: 14.9g
- Carbohydrates: 3.2g
- Fat: 18g
- Fiber: 1.1g

23. Bell Pepper Frittata

Preparation Time: 10 minutes
Cooking Time: 15 minutes
Servings: 4
Ingredients:

- 1 cup red bell pepper, chopped

- 1 tablespoon olive oil, melted
- 1 tomato, sliced
- 4 eggs, beaten
- ¼ teaspoon ground black pepper
- ¼ teaspoon salt

Directions:
1. Brush the baking pan with melted olive oil. Then add all remaining ingredients, mix gently and transfer in the preheated to 365°F oven. Cook the frittata for 15 minutes.

Nutrition:

- Calories: 105
- Protein: 6g
- Carbohydrates: 3.3g
- Fat: 7.9g
- Fiber: 0.6g

24. Fish Eggs

Preparation Time: 5 minutes
Cooking Time: 20 minutes
Servings: 4
Ingredients:
- 1 cup sweet potato, chopped, cooked
- 1 tablespoon avocado oil
- 10 oz. salmon fillet, chopped
- ¼ cup cauliflower, chopped
- 4 eggs, beaten

Directions:
1. Mash or crush the sweet potato, then mix it with chopped salmon and cauliflower. Then heat avocado oil in the pan.
2. Add mashed sweet potato mixture and cook it for 10 minutes. Stir to from time to time.
3. After this, add eggs, whisk the mixture gently. Close the lid and cook it for 10 more minutes.

Nutrition:

- Calories: 208
- Protein: 20.5g
- Carbohydrates: 11.2g
- Fat: 9.3g
- Fiber: 2g

Chapter 4. Lunch Recipes

25. Salmon Stew

Preparation Time: 8 minutes
Cooking Time: 12 minutes
Servings: 2
Ingredients:

- 1-pound salmon fillet, sliced
- 1 onion, chopped
- Salt, to taste
- 1 tablespoon butter, melted
- 1 cup fish broth
- ½ teaspoon red chili powder

Directions:

1. Season the salmon fillets with salt and red chili powder.
2. Put butter and onions in a skillet and sauté for about 3 minutes.
3. Add seasoned salmon and cook for about 2 minutes on each side.
4. Add fish broth and secure the lid.
5. Cook for about 7 minutes on medium heat and open the lid.
6. Dish out and serve immediately.
7. Transfer the stew to a bowl and set aside to cool for meal prepping. Divide the mixture into 2 containers. Cover the containers and refrigerate for about 2 days. Reheat in the microwave before serving.

Nutrition:

- Calories: 272
- Carbs: 4.4g
- Protein: 32.1g
- Fat: 14.2g
- Sugar: 1.9g

26. Asparagus Salmon Fillets

Preparation Time: 10 minutes
Cooking Time: 20 minutes
Servings: 2
Ingredients:

- 1 teaspoon olive oil
- 4 asparagus stalks
- 2 salmon fillets
- ¼ cup butter
- ¼ cup champagne
- Salt and freshly ground black pepper, to taste

Directions:

1. Preheat the oven to 355 degrees and grease a baking dish.
2. Put all the ingredients in a bowl and mix well.
3. Put this mixture in the baking dish and transfer it to the oven.
4. Bake for about 20 minutes and dish out.
5. Place the salmon fillets in a dish and set them aside to cool for meal prepping. Divide it into 2 containers and close the lid. Refrigerate for 1 day and reheat in microwave before serving.

Nutrition:

- Calories: 475
- Carbs: 1.1g
- Protein: 35.2g
- Fat: 36.8g
- Sugar: 0.5g
- Sodium: 242mg

27. Crispy Baked Chicken

Preparation Time: 30 minutes
Cooking Time: 10 minutes
Servings: 2
Ingredients:

- 2 chicken breasts, skinless and boneless
- 2 tablespoons butter
- ¼ teaspoon turmeric powder
- Salt and black pepper, to taste
- ¼ cup sour cream

Directions:

1. Preheat the oven to 360 degrees and grease a baking dish with butter.
2. Season the chicken with turmeric powder, salt, and black pepper in a bowl.
3. Put the chicken on the baking dish and transfer it to the oven.
4. Bake for about 10 minutes and dish out to serve topped with sour cream.
5. Transfer the chicken to a bowl and set aside to cool for meal prepping. Divide it into 2 containers and cover the containers. Refrigerate for up to 2 days and reheat in microwave before serving.

Nutrition:

- Calories: 304
- Carbs: 1.4g
- Protein: 26.1g
- Fat: 21.6g
- Sugar: 0.1g
- Sodium: 137mg

28. Sour and Sweet Fish

Preparation Time: 15 minutes
Cooking Time: 10 minutes
Servings: 2
Ingredients:

- 1 tablespoon vinegar
- 2 drops stevia
- 1-pound fish chunks
- ¼ cup butter, melted
- Salt and black pepper, to taste

Directions:

1. Put butter and fish chunks in a skillet and cook for about 3 minutes.
2. Add stevia, salt and black pepper and cook for about 10 minutes, stirring continuously.
3. Dish out in a bowl and serve immediately.
4. Place fish in a dish and set aside to cool for meal prepping. Divide it into 2 containers and refrigerate for up to 2 days. Reheat in the microwave before serving.

Nutrition:

- Calories: 258
- Carbs: 2.8g
- Protein: 24.5g
- Fat: 16.7g
- Sugar: 2.7g
- Sodium: 649mg

29. Creamy Chicken

Preparation Time: 12 minutes
Cooking Time: 13 minutes
Servings: 2
Ingredients:

- ½ small onion, chopped
- ¼ cup sour cream
- 1 tablespoon butter
- ¼ cup mushrooms
- ½ pound chicken breasts

Directions:

1. Heat butter in a skillet and add onions and mushrooms.
2. Sauté for about 5 minutes and add chicken breasts and salt.
3. Secure the lid and cook for about 5 more minutes.
4. Add sour cream and cook for about 3 minutes.
5. Open the lid and dish it out in a bowl to serve immediately.
6. Transfer the creamy chicken breasts to a dish and set aside to cool for meal prepping. Divide them into 2 containers and cover their lid. Refrigerate for 2-3 days and reheat in microwave before serving.

Nutrition:

- Calories: 335
- Carbs: 2.9g
- Protein: 34g
- Fat: 20.2g
- Sugar: 0.8g
- Sodium: 154mg

30. Paprika Butter Shrimp

Preparation Time: 15 minutes
Cooking Time: 15 minutes
Servings: 2
Ingredients:

- ¼ tablespoon smoked paprika
- 1/8 cup sour cream
- ½ pound shrimp
- 1/8 cup butter
- Salt and black pepper, to taste

Directions:

1. Preheat the oven to 390 degrees and grease a baking dish.
2. Mix together all the ingredients in a large bowl and transfer them into the baking dish.
3. Place in the oven and bake for about 15 minutes.
4. Place paprika shrimp in a dish and set aside to cool for meal prepping. Divide it into 2 containers and cover the lid. Refrigerate for 1-2 days and reheat in microwave before serving.

Nutrition:

- Calories: 330
- Carbs: 1.5g
- Protein: 32.6g
- Fat: 21.5g
- Sugar: 0.2g
- Sodium: 458mg

31. Almond Flour Burger with Goat Cheese

Preparation Time: 10 minutes
Cooking Time: 20 minutes
Servings: 2
Ingredients:

- 2 almond flour bagels
- 2 tbsp. of fresh goat cheese
- 4 slices smoked salmon
- 2 pinch Salt and pepper
- 4 Radishes
- Dill

Directions:

1. Cut the gluten-free bagel in half. Put the two halves in the toaster to make them crisp.
2. Spread both slices of fresh goat cheese and add salmon.
3. Garnish the bagel with radish and dill.
4. A pinch of salt and pepper and its ready
5. Put each burger in a container and store it in the refrigerator

Nutrition:

- Calories: 325
- Fat: 29g
- Carbs: 4g
- Protein 12g
- Sugar: 0.9g

32. Sausage Skillet with Cabbage

Preparation Time: 5 minutes
Cooking Time: 13 minutes
Servings: 2
Ingredients:

- 1 tbsp. olive oil
- 3/4 cup shredded green cabbage
- 3/4 cup grated red cabbage
- 1/4 cup diced onion
- 1/4 cup spicy sausages
- 1/4 cup grated mozzarella
- 1 tbsp. fresh and chopped parsley
- Salt and pepper to taste

Directions:

1. Place a large skillet on a stove over medium-high heat and heat olive oil. Immerse the cabbage and onion in the heated oil. Let stand for about 8-10 minutes or until vegetables are tender.
2. Chop the sausage into bite-size pieces. Mix with cabbage and onion and let stand another 8 minutes.
3. Spread the cheese over the top
4. Cover the skillet with a lid and set aside for 5 minutes to melt.
5. Remove the lid and mix your ingredients. Garnish with salt, pepper, and parsley before serving.
6. To assemble the dish, divide the mixture between 2 containers; then store it in the refrigerator

Nutrition:

- Calories: 316
- Fat: 27.2g
- Carbs: 4.9g
- Protein 12.8g
- Sugar: 1.3g

33. Chicken and Broccoli Gratin

Preparation Time: 10 minutes
Cooking Time: 10 minutes
Servings: 2
Ingredients:

- 1pound of chicken breasts
- 1/4 cup almond butter
- 100 cl of fresh cream
- 1 cup goat cheese
- 2 organic eggs
- 2 Crushed garlic cloves
- 1 pinch of salt
- 1 Pinch of pepper

Directions:

1. Cook the broccoli in a pot of water for 10 minutes. It must remain firm.
2. Melt the butter in a skillet; add the crushed garlic clove and the salted and peppered chicken. Let it get a brown color.
3. Drain the broccoli and mix with the chicken.
4. Beat the eggs with cream, salt, and pepper. Place broccoli and chicken in a baking dish, cover with cream mixture and sprinkle with grated cheese.
5. Put in the oven at 390°F for 20 minutes.
6. When the gratin is ready; set it aside to cool for 3 minutes
7. Cut the gratin into two halves or in four portions
8. Place every two portions of gratin in a container so that you have two containers.

Nutrition:

- Calories: 612
- Fat: 48g
- Carbs: 11g
- Protein 34g

34. Chicken Curry

Preparation Time: 10 minutes
Cooking Time: 30 minutes
Servings: 2
Ingredients:

- 2 chicken breasts
- 1garlic clove
- 1 small onion
- 1 zucchini
- 2 carrots
- 1 box of bamboo shoots or sprouts
- 1 cup coconut milk
- 1 Tbsp. tomato paste
- 2 tbsps. yellow curry paste

Directions:

1. Mince the onion and sauté in a pan with a little oil for a few minutes.
2. Add chicken cut in large cubes and crushed garlic, salt, pepper and sauté quickly over high heat until meat begins to color.
3. Pour zucchini and carrots in thick slices into the pan.
4. Sear over high heat for a few minutes, then add the coconut milk, tomato sauce, bamboo shoots and one to two tbsps. curry paste, depending on your taste.
5. Cook over low heat and cover for 30 to 45 minutes, stirring occasionally
6. Once cooked, divide the chicken curry between 2 containers
7. Store the containers in the refrigerator

Nutrition:

- Calories: 626
- Fat: 53.2g
- Carbs: 9g
- Protein: 27.8g

35. Bacon Wrapped Asparagus

Preparation Time: 10 minutes
Cooking Time: 20 minutes
Servings: 2
Ingredients:

- 1/3 cup heavy whipping cream
- 2 bacon slices, precooked
- 4 small spears asparagus
- Salt, to taste
- 1 tablespoon butter

Directions:

1. Preheat the oven to 360 degrees and grease a baking sheet with butter.
2. Meanwhile, mix cream, asparagus and salt in a bowl.
3. Wrap the asparagus in bacon slices and arrange them in the baking dish.
4. Transfer the baking dish to the oven and bake for about 20 minutes.
5. Remove from the oven and serve hot.
6. Place the bacon-wrapped asparagus in a dish and set it aside to cool for meal prepping. Divide it into 2 containers and cover the lid. Refrigerate for about 2 days and reheat in the microwave before serving.

Nutrition:

- Calories: 204
- Carbs: 1.4g
- Protein: 5.9g
- Fat: 19.3g
- Sugar: 0.5g

36. Spinach Chicken

Preparation Time: 10 minutes
Cooking Time: 10 minutes
Servings: 2
Ingredients:

- 2garlic cloves, minced
- 2 tablespoons unsalted butter, divided
- ¼ cup parmesan cheese, shredded
- ¾ pound chicken tenders
- ¼ cup heavy cream
- 10 ounces frozen spinach, chopped
- Salt and black pepper, to taste

Directions:

1. Heat 1 tablespoon of butter in a large skillet and add chicken, salt, and black pepper.
2. Cook for about 3 minutes on both sides and remove the chicken to a bowl.
3. Melt remaining butter in the skillet and add garlic, cheese, heavy cream, and spinach.
4. Cook for about 2 minutes and add the chicken.
5. Cook for about 5 minutes on low heat and dish out to immediately serve.
6. Place chicken in a dish and set aside to cool for meal prepping. Divide it into 2 containers and cover them. Refrigerate for about 3 days and reheat in microwave before serving.

Nutrition:

- Calories: 288
- Carbs: 3.6g
- Protein: 27.7g
- Fat: 18.3g
- Sugar: 0.3g

37. Lemongrass Prawns

Preparation Time: 10 minutes
Cooking Time: 15 minutes
Servings: 2
Ingredients:

- ½ red chili pepper, seeded and chopped
- 2 lemongrass stalks
- ½ pound prawns, deveined and peeled
- 6 tablespoons butter
- ¼ teaspoon smoked paprika

Directions:

1. Preheat the oven to 390 degrees and grease a baking dish.
2. Mix together red chili pepper, butter, smoked paprika, and prawns in a bowl.
3. Marinate for about 2 hours and then thread the prawns on the lemongrass stalks.
4. Arrange the threaded prawns on the baking dish and transfer them to the oven.
5. Bake for about 15 minutes and dish out to serve immediately.
6. Place the prawns in a dish and set them aside to cool for meal prepping. Divide it into 2 containers and close the lid. Refrigerate for about 4 days and reheat in microwave before serving.

Nutrition:

- Calories: 322
- Carbs: 3.8g
- Protein: 34.8g
- Fat: 18g
- Sugar: 0.1g
- Sodium: 478mg

38. Stuffed Mushrooms

Preparation Time: 20 minutes
Cooking Time: 25 minutes
Servings: 4
Ingredients:

- 2 ounces' bacon, crumbled
- ½ tablespoon butter
- ¼ teaspoon paprika powder
- 2 Portobello mushrooms
- 1 oz. cream cheese
- ¾ tablespoon fresh chives, chopped
- Salt and black pepper, to taste

Directions:

1. Preheat the oven to 400 degrees and grease a baking dish.
2. Heat butter in a skillet and add mushrooms.
3. Sauté for about 4 minutes and set aside.
4. Mix together cream cheese, chives, paprika powder, salt, and black pepper in a bowl.
5. Stuff the mushrooms with this mixture and transfer them to the baking dish.
6. Place in the oven and bake for about 20 minutes.
7. These mushrooms can be refrigerated for about 3 days for meal prepping and can be served with scrambled eggs.

Nutrition:

- Calories: 570
- Carbs: 4.6g
- Protein: 19.9g
- Fat: 52.8g
- Sugar: 0.8g
- Sodium: 1041mg

39. Honey Glazed Chicken Drumsticks

Preparation Time: 10 minutes
Cooking Time: 20 minutes
Servings: 2
Ingredients:

- ½ tablespoon fresh thyme, minced
- 1/8 cup Dijon mustard
- ½ tablespoon fresh rosemary, minced
- ½ tablespoon honey
- 2 chicken drumsticks
- 1 tablespoon olive oil
- Salt and black pepper, to taste

Directions:

1. Preheat the oven at 325 degrees and grease a baking dish.
2. Combine all the ingredients in a bowl except the drumsticks and mix well.
3. Add drumsticks and coat generously with the mixture.
4. Cover and refrigerate to marinate overnight.
5. Place the drumsticks in the baking dish and transfer them to the oven.
6. Cook for about 20 minutes and dish out to immediately serve.
7. Place chicken drumsticks in a dish and set them aside to cool for meal prepping. Divide it into 2 containers and cover them. Refrigerate for about 3 days and reheat in microwave before serving.

Nutrition:

- Calories: 301
- Carbs: 6g
- Fats: 19.7g
- Proteins: 4.5g
- Sugar: 4.5g
- Sodium: 316mg

40. Keto Zucchini Pizza

Preparation Time: 10 minutes
Cooking Time: 15 minutes
Servings: 2
Ingredients:

- 1/8 cup spaghetti sauce
- ½ zucchini, cut in circular slices
- ½ cup cream cheese
- Pepperoni slices, for topping
- ½ cup mozzarella cheese, shredded

Directions:

1. Preheat the oven to 350 degrees and grease a baking dish.
2. Arrange the zucchini on the baking dish and layer with spaghetti sauce.
3. Top with pepperoni slices and mozzarella cheese.
4. Transfer the baking dish to the oven and bake for about 15 minutes.
5. Remove from the oven and serve immediately.

Nutrition:

- Calories: 445
- Carbs: 3.6g
- Protein: 12.8g
- Fat: 42g
- Sugar: 0.3g
- Sodium: 429mg

41. Omega-3 Salad

Preparation Time: 10 minutes
Cooking Time: 5 minutes
Servings: 2
Ingredients:

- ½ pound skinless salmon fillet, cut into 4 steaks
- ¼ tablespoon fresh lime juice
- 1 tablespoon olive oil, divided
- 4 tablespoons sour cream
- ¼ zucchini, cut into small cubes
- ¼ teaspoon jalapeño pepper, seeded and chopped finely
- Salt and black pepper, to taste
- ¼ tablespoon fresh dill, chopped

Directions:

1. Put olive oil and salmon in a skillet and cook for about 5 minutes on both sides.
2. Season with salt and black pepper, stirring well, and dish out.
3. Mix remaining ingredients in a bowl and add cooked salmon to serve.

Nutrition:

- Calories: 291
- Fat: 21.1g
- Carbs: 2.5g
- Protein: 23.1g
- Sugar: 0.6g
- Sodium: 112mg

42. Crab Cakes

Preparation Time: 20 minutes
Cooking Time: 10 minutes
Servings: 2
Ingredients:

- ½ pound lump crabmeat, drained
- 2 tablespoons coconut flour
- 1 tablespoon mayonnaise
- ¼ teaspoon green Tabasco sauce
- 3 tablespoons butter
- 1 small egg, beaten
- ¾ tablespoon fresh parsley, chopped
- ½ teaspoon yellow mustard
- Salt and black pepper, to taste

Directions:

1. Mix together all the ingredients in a bowl except butter.
2. Make patties from this mixture and set them aside.
3. Heat butter in a skillet over medium heat and add patties.
4. Cook for about 10 minutes on each side and dish out to serve hot.
5. You can store the raw patties in the freezer for about 3 weeks for meal prepping. Place patties in a container and place parchment paper in between the patties to avoid stickiness.

Nutrition:

- Calories: 153
- Fat: 10.8g
- Carbs: 6.7g
- Protein: 6.4g
- Sugar: 2.4
- Sodium: 46mg

43. Salmon Burgers

Preparation Time: 17 minutes
Cooking Time: 3 minutes
Servings: 2
Ingredients:

- 1 tablespoon sugar-free ranch dressing
- ½-ounce smoked salmon, chopped roughly
- ½ tablespoon fresh parsley, chopped
- ½ tablespoon avocado oil
- 1 small egg
- 4-ounce pink salmon, drained and bones removed
- 1/8 cup almond flour
- ¼ teaspoon Cajun seasoning

Directions:

1. Mix together all the ingredients in a bowl and stir well.
2. Make patties from this mixture and set them aside.
3. Heat a skillet over medium heat and add patties.
4. Cook for about 3 minutes per side and dish out to serve.
5. You can store the raw patties in the freezer for about 3 weeks for meal prepping. Place patties in a container and place parchment paper in between the patties to avoid stickiness.

Nutrition:

- Calories: 59
- Fat: 12.7g
- Carbs: 2.4g
- Protein: 6.3g
- Sugar: 0.7g
- Sodium: 25mg

Chapter 5. Dinner Recipes

44. Pork in Blue Cheese Sauce

Preparation time: 15 minutes
Cooking time: 30 minutes
Servings: 6
Ingredients:

- 2 pounds' pork center-cut loin roast, boneless and cut into 6 pieces
- 1 tablespoon coconut amino
- 6 ounces' blue cheese
- 1/3 cup heavy cream
- 1/3 cup port wine
- 1/3 cup roasted vegetable broth, preferably homemade
- 1 teaspoon dried hot Chile flake
- 1 teaspoon dried rosemary
- 1 tablespoon lard

- 1 shallot, chopped
- 2garlic cloves, chopped
- Salt
- Cracked black peppercorns

Directions:

1. Rub each piece of the pork with salt, black peppercorns, and rosemary.
2. Melt the lard in a saucepan over a moderately high flame. Sear the pork on all sides for about 15 minutes; set aside.
3. Cook the shallot and garlic until they've softened. Add in port wine to scrape up any brown bits from the bottom.
4. Adjust to medium-low, add in the remaining ingredients; continue to simmer until the sauce has thickened and reduced.

Nutrition:

- Calories: 34
- Fat: 18.9g
- Carbs: 1.9g
- Protein: 40.3g
- Fiber: 0.3g

45. Mississippi Pulled Pork

Preparation Time: 15 minutes
Cooking Time: 6 hours
Servings: 4
Ingredients:

- 1 ½ pound pork shoulder
- 1 tablespoon liquid smoke sauce
- 1 teaspoon chipotle powder
- Au Jus gravy seasoning packet
- 2 onions, cut into wedges
- Kosher salt
- Ground black pepper

Directions:

1. Mix the liquid smoke sauce, chipotle powder, Au Jus gravy seasoning packet, salt, and pepper. Massage the spice mixture into the pork on all sides.
2. Wrap in plastic wrap and let it marinate in your refrigerator for 3 hours.
3. Prepare your grill for indirect heat. Place the pork butt roast on the grate over a drip pan and top with onions; cover the grill and cook for about 6 hours.
4. Transfer the pork to a cutting board. Now, shred the meat into bite-sized pieces using two forks.

Nutrition:

- Calories: 350
- Fat: 11g
- Carbs: 5g
- Protein: 53.6g
- Fiber: 2.2g

46. Spicy and Cheesy Turkey Dip

Preparation Time: 15 minutes
Cooking Time: 25 minutes
Servings: 4
Ingredients:
- 1 Fresno chili pepper, deveined and minced
- 1 ½ cups Ricotta cheese, creamed, 4% fat, softened
- 1/4 cup sour cream
- 1 tablespoon butter, room temperature
- 1 shallot, chopped
- 1 teaspoon garlic, pressed
- 1-pound ground turkey
- 1/2 cup goat cheese, shredded
- Salt and black pepper, to taste
- 1 ½ cups Gruyere, shredded

Directions:
1. Dissolve the butter in a frying pan over a moderately high flame. Now, sauté the onion and garlic until they have softened.
2. Stir in the ground turkey and continue to cook until it is no longer pink.
3. Transfer the sautéed mixture to a lightly greased baking dish. Add in Ricotta, sour cream, goat cheese, salt, pepper, and chili pepper.
4. Top with the shredded Gruyere cheese. Bake at 350 degrees F within 20 minutes in the preheated oven or until hot and bubbly on top.

Nutrition:

- Calories: 284
- Fat: 19g
- Carbs: 3.2g
- Protein: 26g
- Fiber: 1.6g

47. Turkey Chorizo with Bok Choy

Preparation Time: 15 minutes
Cooking Time: 50 minutes
Servings: 4
Ingredients:

- 4 mild turkey Chorizo, sliced
- 1/2 cup full-fat milk
- 6 ounces Gruyere cheese, preferably freshly grated
- 1 yellow onion, chopped
- Coarse salt
- Ground black pepper
- 1-pound Bok choy, tough stem ends trimmed
- 1 cup cream of mushroom soup
- 1 tablespoon lard, room temperature

Directions:

1. Melt the lard in a nonstick skillet over a moderate flame; cook the Chorizo sausage for about 5 minutes, occasionally stirring to ensure even cooking; reserve.
2. Add in the onion, salt, pepper, Bok choy, and cream of mushroom soup. Continue to cook for 4 minutes longer or until the vegetables have softened.
3. Put the batter into a lightly oiled casserole dish. Top with the reserved Chorizo.
4. In a mixing bowl, thoroughly combine the milk and cheese. Pour the cheese mixture over the sausage.
5. Cover with foil and bake at 36degrees F for about 35 minutes.

Nutrition:

- Calories: 18
- Fat: 12g
- Carbs: 2.6g
- Protein: 9.4g
- Fiber: 1g

48. Spicy Chicken Breasts

Preparation Time: 15 minutes
Cooking Time: 30 minutes
Servings: 6
Ingredients:

- 1 ½ pounds chicken breasts
- 1 bell pepper, deveined and chopped
- 1 leek, chopped
- 1 tomato, pureed
- 2 tablespoons coriander
- 2garlic cloves, minced
- 1 teaspoon cayenne pepper
- 1 teaspoon dry thyme
- 1/4 cup coconut amino
- Sea salt
- Ground black pepper

Directions:

1. Rub each chicken breasts with garlic, cayenne pepper, thyme, salt, and black pepper. Cook the chicken in a saucepan over medium-high heat.
2. Sear for about 5 minutes until golden brown on all sides. Fold in the tomato puree and coconut amino and bring it to a boil. Add in the pepper, leek, and coriander.
3. Reduce the heat to simmer. Continue to cook, partially covered, for about 20 minutes.

Nutrition:

- Calories: 239
- Fat: 6g
- Carbs: 5.5g
- Protein: 34.3g
- Fiber: 1g

49. Saucy Boston Butt

Preparation Time: 15 minutes
Cooking Time: 1 hour 20 minutes
Servings: 8
Ingredients:

- 1 tablespoon lard, room temperature
- 2 pounds Boston butt, cubed
- Salt and freshly ground pepper
- 1/2 teaspoon mustard powder
- A bunch of spring onions, chopped
- 2garlic cloves, minced
- 1/2 tablespoon ground cardamom
- 2 tomatoes, pureed
- 1 bell pepper, deveined and chopped
- 1 jalapeno pepper, deveined and finely chopped
- 1/2 cup unsweetened coconut milk
- 2 cups of chicken bone broth

Directions:

1. In a wok, melt the lard over moderate heat. Massage the pork belly with salt, pepper, and mustard powder.
2. Sear the pork for 8 to 10 minutes, stirring periodically to ensure cooking; set aside, and keep it warm.
3. In the same wok, sauté the spring onions, garlic, and cardamom. Spoon the sautéed vegetables along with the reserved pork into the slow cooker.
4. Add in the remaining ingredients, cover with the lid and cook for 1 hour 10 minutes over low heat.

Nutrition:

- Calories: 369
- Fat: 20.2g
- Carbs: 2.9g
- Protein: 41.3g
- Fiber: 0.7g

50. Old-Fashioned Goulash

Preparation Time: 15 minutes
Cooking Time: 9 hours 10 minutes
Servings: 4
Ingredients:
- 1 ½ pound pork butt, chopped
- 1 teaspoon sweet Hungarian paprika
- 2 Hungarian hot peppers, deveined and minced
- 1 cup leeks, chopped
- 1 ½ tablespoons lard
- 1 teaspoon caraway seeds, ground
- 4 cups vegetable broth
- 2garlic cloves, crushed
- 1 teaspoon cayenne pepper
- 2 cups tomato sauce with herbs
- 1 ½ pound pork butt, chopped
- 1 teaspoon sweet Hungarian paprika
- 2 Hungarian hot peppers, deveined and minced
- 1 cup leeks, chopped
- 1 ½ tablespoons lard
- 1 teaspoon caraway seeds, ground
- 4 cups vegetable broth
- 2garlic cloves, crushed
- 1 teaspoon cayenne pepper
- 2 cups tomato sauce with herbs

Directions:
1. Melt the lard in a heavy-bottomed pot over medium-high heat. Sear the pork for 5 to 6 minutes until just browned on all sides; set aside.
2. Add in the leeks and garlic; continue to cook until they have softened.
3. Place the reserved pork along with the sautéed mixture in your crockpot. Put in the other fixings and stir to combine.
4. Cover with the lid and slow cook for 9 hours on the lowest setting.

Nutrition:

- Calories: 456
- Fat: 27g
- Carbs: 6.7g
- Protein: 32g
- Fiber: 3.4g

51. Flatbread with Chicken Liver Pâté

Preparation Time: 15 minutes
Cooking Time: 2 hours 15 minutes
Servings: 4
Ingredients:
- 1 yellow onion, finely chopped
- 10 ounces' chicken livers
- 1/2 teaspoon Mediterranean seasoning blend
- 4 tablespoons olive oil
- 1garlic clove, minced

For Flatbread:
- 1 cup lukewarm water
- 1/2 stick butter
- 1/2 cup flax meal
- 1 ½ tablespoons psyllium husks
- 1 ¼ cups almond flour

Directions:
1. Pulse the chicken livers along with the seasoning blend, olive oil, onion, and garlic in your food processor; reserve.
2. Mix the dry ingredients for the flatbread. Mix in all the wet ingredients. Whisk to combine well.
3. Set aside at room temperature within 2 hours. Split the dough into 8 balls and roll them out on a flat surface.
4. In a lightly greased pan, cook your flatbread for 1 minute on each side or until golden.

Nutrition:

- Calories: 395
- Fat: 30.2g

- Carbs: 3.6g
- Protein: 17.9g
- Fiber: 0.5g

52. Sunday Chicken with Cauliflower Salad

Preparation Time: 15 minutes
Cooking Time: 20 minutes
Servings: 2
Ingredients:
- 1 teaspoon hot paprika
- 2 tablespoons fresh basil, snipped
- 1/2 cup mayonnaise
- 1 teaspoon mustard
- 2 teaspoons butter
- 2 chicken wings
- 1/2 cup cheddar cheese, shredded
- Sea salt
- Ground black pepper
- 2 tablespoons dry sherry
- 1 shallot, finely minced
- 1/2 head of cauliflower

Directions:
1. Boil the cauliflower with salted water in a pot until it has softened; cut into small florets and place in a salad bowl.
2. Melt the butter in a saucepan over medium-high heat. Cook the chicken for about 8 minutes or until the skin is crisp and browned. Season with hot paprika salt, and black pepper.
3. Whisk the mayonnaise, mustard, dry sherry, and shallot, and dress your salad. Top with cheddar cheese and fresh basil.

Nutrition:

- Calories: 444
- Fat: 36g
- Carbs: 5.7g

- Protein: 20.6g
- Fiber: 4.3g

53. Authentic Turkey Kebabs

Preparation Time: 15 minutes
Cooking Time: 30 minutes
Servings: 6
Ingredients:
- 1 ½ pounds turkey breast, cubed
- 3 Spanish peppers, sliced
- 2 zucchinis, cut into thick slices
- 1 onion, cut into wedges
- 2 tablespoons olive oil, room temperature
- 1 tablespoon dry ranch seasoning

Directions:
1. Thread the turkey pieces and vegetables onto bamboo skewers. Sprinkle the skewers with dry ranch seasoning and olive oil.
2. Grill your kebabs for about 10 minutes, turning them periodically to ensure even cooking.
3. Wrap your kebabs in foil before packing them into airtight containers; keep them in your refrigerator for up to 3 days.

Nutrition:

- Calories: 2
- Fat: 13.8g
- Carbs: 6.7g
- Protein: 25.8g
- Fiber: 1.2g

54. Mexican-Style Turkey Bacon Bites

Preparation Time: 5 minutes
Cooking Time: 0 minutes
Servings: 8
Ingredients:
- 4 ounces' turkey bacon, chopped
- 4 ounces Neufchatel cheese
- 1 tablespoon butter, cold
- 1 jalapeno pepper, deveined and minced
- 1 teaspoon Mexican oregano
- 2 tablespoons scallions, finely chopped

Directions:
1. Mix all the fixings in a mixing bowl. Roll the mixture into 8 balls. Serve.

Nutrition:

- Calories: 19
- Fat: 16.7g
- Carbs: 2.2g
- Protein: 8.8g
- Fiber: 0.3g

55. Easy Fall-off-the-Bone Ribs

Preparation Time: 15 minutes
Cooking Time: 8 hours
Servings: 4
Ingredients:
- 1-pound baby back ribs
- 4 tablespoons coconut amino
- 1/4 cup dry red wine
- 1/2 teaspoon cayenne pepper
- 1garlic clove, crushed
- 1 teaspoon Italian herb mix

- 1 tablespoon butter
- 1 teaspoon Serrano pepper, minced
- 1 Italian pepper, thinly sliced
- 1 teaspoon grated lemon zest

Directions:
1. Grease the sides and bottom of the crockpot. Place the pork and peppers on the bottom.
2. Add in the remaining ingredients. Slow cook for 9 hours on a low heat setting.

Nutrition:

- Calories: 192
- Fat: 6.9g
- Carbs: 0.9g
- Protein: 29.8g
- Fiber: 0.5g

56. Brie-Stuffed Meatballs

Preparation Time: 15 minutes
Cooking Time: 25 minutes
Servings: 5
Ingredients:
- 2 eggs, beaten
- 1-pound ground pork
- 1/3 cup double cream
- 1 tablespoon fresh parsley
- Kosher salt and ground black pepper
- 1 teaspoon dried rosemary
- 10 (1-inch cubes) of brie cheese
- 2 tablespoons scallions, minced
- 2 cloves garlic, minced

Directions:
1. Mix all ingredients, except for the brie cheese, until everything is well incorporated.

2. Roll the mixture into 10 patties. Place cheese in the center of each patty and roll into a ball—roast in the preheated oven at 0 degrees F for about 20 minutes.

Nutrition:

- Calories: 302
- Fat: 13g
- Carbs: 1.9g
- Protein: 33.4g
- Fiber: 0.3g

57. Roasted Leg Lamb

Preparation Time: 15 minutes
Cooking Time: 2 hours & 30 minutes
Servings: 12
Ingredients:
- 1-112 to 144 ounces' bone-in lamb leg, trimmed

- 1 cup of chicken broth

Marinade:

- 1/3 cup fresh minced rosemary
- 2 tablespoons of Dijon mustard
- 2 tablespoons of olive oil
- 8 minced garlic cloves
- 1 teaspoon soy sauce reduced-sodium
- 1/2 teaspoon salt
- 1/2 teaspoon pepper

Directions:

1. Preheat your oven to 325°F.
2. Combine marinade ingredients and coat the lamb. Refrigerate with cover overnight.
3. Place the lamb on a rack using a shallow roasting pan with the fat side up.
4. Bake without cover for 1 ½ hour.
5. Pour the broth, then cover loosely using foil. Bake for another 1 ½ hours or until meat turns to your desired doneness.
6. Let the lamb cool for 10 to 15 minutes before slicing.

Nutrition:

- Calories: 246
- Carbohydrates: 2g
- Fiber: 0g
- Fats: 11g
- Sodium: 320 mg
- Protein: 33g

58. Lamb Chops Curry

Preparation Time: 15 minutes
Cooking Time: 30 minutes
Servings: 2
Ingredients:

- 4-4 ounces' bone-in loin chops of lamb
- 1 tablespoon of canola oil
- 3/4 cup of orange juice
- 2 tablespoons teriyaki sauce reduced-sodium
- 2 teaspoons of grated orange zest
- 1 teaspoon of curry powder
- 1garlic clove, minced
- 1 teaspoon cornstarch
- 2 tablespoons of cold water

Directions:

1. Brown lamb chops on both sides over canola oil.
2. Combine the other five ingredients and pour them over the skillet. Cover and let it simmer for 15 to 20 minutes or until lamb turns tender. Remove from heat and keep warm.
3. Combine the last two ingredients until smooth. Mix into the pan drippings and boil for 2 minutes or until it thickens.
4. Serve with steamed rice if desired.

Nutrition:

- Calories: 337
- Carbohydrates: 15g
- Fiber: 1g
- Fats: 17g
- Sodium: 402 mg
- Protein: 30g

59. Pork Cutlets in Cucumber Sauce

Preparation Time: 4 hours & 15 minutes
Cooking Time: 15 minutes
Servings: 4
Ingredients:
Marinade:

- 16 ounces' pork tenderloin, cut into ½-inch thick slices
- 1 small chopped onion
- 2 tablespoons of lemon juice
- 1 tablespoon fresh minced parsley
- 2 minced garlic cloves
- 3/4 teaspoon of dried thyme
- 1/8 teaspoon pepper

Cucumber Sauce:

- 1 small seeded and chopped tomato
- 2/3 cup plain yogurt, reduced-fat
- 1/2 cup seeded cucumber, chopped
- 1 tablespoon onion, finely chopped
- 1/2 teaspoon of lemon juice
- 1/8 teaspoon of garlic powder

Directions:

1. Mix all the marinade fixings and marinate the chops for 4 hours (or overnight). Cover and refrigerate.
2. Combine all the cucumber sauce ingredients and mix. Cover and refrigerate.
3. Drain and discard marinade—place chops on a greased broiler pan. Broil for 6 to 8 minutes, each side 4-inch from the heat. Serve with cucumber sauce.

Nutrition:

- Calories: 177
- Carbohydrates: 8g
- Fiber: 1g
- Fats: 5g
- Sodium: 77 mg

60. Grilled Lamb Chops

Preparation Time: 4 hours & 15 minutes
Cooking Time: 15 minutes
Servings: 4
Ingredients:
- 8-3 ounces' lamb loin chops

Marinade:
- 1 small sliced onion
- 2 tablespoons of red wine vinegar
- 1 tablespoon of lemon juice
- 1 tablespoon of olive oil
- 2 teaspoons fresh minced rosemary (substitute 3/4 tsp. crushed dried)
- 2 teaspoons of Dijon mustard
- 1 minced garlic clove
- 1/2 teaspoon pepper
- 1/4 teaspoon salt
- 1/4 teaspoon of ground ginger

Directions:
1. Coat the lamb chops with the combined marinade mixture. Cover and refrigerate for 4 hours or overnight.
2. Drain and discard marinade. Lightly oil your grill rack.
3. Grill lamb chops for 4 to 7 minutes on each side over medium heat. Serve.

Nutrition:

- Calories: 164
- Carbohydrates: 0g
- Fiber: 0g
- Fats: 8g
- Sodium: 112 mg
- Protein: 21g

61. Pork and Orzo in a Bowl

Preparation Time: 15 minutes
Cooking Time: 30 minutes
Servings: 6
Ingredients:

- 24 ounces of pork tenderloin
- 1 teaspoon of coarsely ground pepper
- 2 tablespoons of olive oil
- 3 quarts' water
- 1-1/4 cups orzo pasta, uncooked
- 1/4 teaspoon salt
- 1-6 ounces package fresh baby spinach
- 1 cup halved grape tomatoes
- 3/4 cup feta cheese, crumbled

Directions:

1. Rub pepper onto the pork; slice into an inch size cube. Warm-up oil on medium heat in a large nonstick skillet and stir-cook pork for 8 to 10 minutes.
2. Meanwhile, boil water and cook the orzo. Add salt. Keep uncovered and cook for 8 minutes. Add in the spinach and cook until orzo turns tender (about 45 to 60 seconds). Drain.
3. Add tomatoes and heat through. Stir in the orzo and cheese.

Nutrition:

- Calories: 372
- Carbohydrates: 34g
- Fiber: 3g
- Fats: 11g
- Sodium: 306 mg
- Protein: 31g

62. Pork Medallion in Lemon Caper Sauce

Preparation Time: 5 minutes
Cooking Time: 30 minutes
Servings: 4
Ingredients:

- 1-16 ounces' pork tenderloin, cut into 12 slices and flatten ¼-inch thick
- 1/2 cup of all-purpose flour
- 1/2 teaspoon salt
- 1/4 teaspoon pepper
- 1 tablespoon butter
- 1 tablespoon of olive oil

Sauce:

- 1 cup chicken broth, reduced-sodium
- 1/4 cup white wine (or ¼ cup reduced-sodium chicken broth)
- 1 minced garlic clove, minced
- 1 tablespoon drained capers
- 1 tablespoon of lemon juice
- 1/2 teaspoon crushed dried rosemary

Directions:

1. Coat pork slices in flour, pepper, and salt mixture.
2. Cook pork slices in batches using oil and butter mixture until juices cleared. Remove from skillet and keep warm.
3. Combine the first three ingredients in the same pan.
4. Stir to loosen brown bits. Bring to a boil until reduced in half, then stir in the remaining ingredients until heated through. Serve with pork.

Nutrition:

- Calories: 232
- Carbohydrates: 7g
- Fiber: 0g
- Fats: 10g
- Sodium: 589 mg
- Protein: 24g

63. Festive Season Stuffed Tenderloin

Preparation Time: 15 minutes
Cooking Time: 60 minutes
Servings: 8
Ingredients:

- 4 teaspoons of olive oil, divided
- 2 minced shallots
- 1-8-ounce package sliced cremini mushrooms
- 3 minced garlic cloves, divided
- 1 tablespoon fresh thyme, chopped (add extra for garnish)
- 1 1/2 teaspoons fresh parsley, chopped (add extra for garnish)
- 1/4 cup dry sherry (or you can use red wine vinegar)
- 32 to 40 ounces' beef tenderloin
- 1/2 cup bread crumbs, fresh whole wheat
- 1 teaspoon salt
- 1/2 teaspoon of black pepper

Directions:

1. Preheat your oven to 425°F.
2. Warm 2 tablespoons oil on medium heat and cook shallots for 5 minutes or until tender. Add mushrooms and stir-cook until it softens (about 8 minutes).
3. Mix in the garlic plus herbs and cook for a minute more before adding the dry sherry. Reduce the sherry by half, then remove and let it cool.
4. Cut the beef lengthwise resembling butterfly wings. Cover with plastic and pound using a mallet until ½-inch thick.
5. Stir in breadcrumbs in your mushroom mixture before spreading evenly onto the beef. Leave a 1-inch space around the edge.
6. Roll the beef jellyroll style and secure with kitchen string at the one-inch interval. Place the rolled meat on a rack inside a shallow roasting pan.
7. Mix the rest of the fixings and rub over the beef—roast beef for 35-40 minutes for medium-rare or according to your desired doneness.
8. Let it cool 15-20 minutes with loosely tented foil before carving. Serve with extra thyme and parsley.

Nutrition:

- Calories: 195
- Carbohydrates: 5g
- Fiber: 1g
- Fats: 9g
- Sodium: 381 mg
- Protein: 21g

64. Italian Pork Loin

Preparation Time: 15 minutes
Cooking Time: 2 hours & 20 minutes
Servings: 2
Ingredients:
- 1-40 ounces trimmed pork loin
- 1 teaspoon of kosher salt
- 3 cloves crushed and peeled garlic
- 2 tablespoons of extra-virgin olive oil
- 2 tablespoons fresh rosemary, chopped
- 1 tablespoon lemon zest, freshly grated
- 3/4 cup of dry vermouth (or substitute with white wine)
- 2 tablespoons of white wine vinegar

Directions:
1. Tie the loin with a kitchen string on two sides and the middle so it will not flatten.
2. Mash the salt and garlic to make a paste. Stir in the other ingredients except for the vermouth and the vinegar. Rub the mixture all over the loin and refrigerate without cover for an hour.
3. Roast loin at a preheated temperature of 375°F, turning it over once or twice for 40 to 50 minutes. Move it into a cutting board and let it cool for 10 minutes.
4. While cooling, pour the vermouth and vinegar into your roasting pan over medium-high temperature. Simmer for 2 to 4 minutes, scraping off the brown bits and reducing the liquid to half.
5. Remove string and slice the roast. Add excess juice to the sauce and serve.

Nutrition:

- Calories: 182
- Carbohydrates: 0.6g
- Fiber: 0.1g
- Fats: 8.3g
- Sodium: 149 mg
- Protein: 20.6g

65. Mediterranean Chili Beef

Preparation Time: 15 minutes
Cooking Time: 25 minutes
Servings: 4
Ingredients:
- 8 ounces' lean ground beef
- 4 minced garlic cloves
- 3/4 teaspoon of salt, divided
- 1/4 teaspoon pepper
- 3 teaspoons of olive oil, divided
- 1 medium sliced red onion
- 2 medium zucchinis, sliced
- 1 medium-size green pepper
- 1-28 ounces can dice tomatoes, undrained
- 1 teaspoon of red wine vinegar
- 1 teaspoon of dried basil
- 1 teaspoon of dried thyme

Directions:
1. Sauté beef in ¼-teaspoon salt, garlic, pepper, and a teaspoon of oil over medium heat until beef turns brown. Drain and remove. Keep warm.
2. Using the same skillet, pour the remaining oil and sauté onion. Add zucchini and green pepper and stir-cook for 4 to 6 minutes until crisp-tender.

3. Stir in the remaining ingredients. Add beef and cook until heated through—suggested serving over pasta or brown rice.

Nutrition:

- Calories: 204
- Carbohydrates: 18g
- Fiber: 6g
- Fats: 9g
- Sodium: 739 mg
- Protein: 15g

66. Cherry Sauce Meatballs

Preparation Time: 30 minutes
Cooking Time: 15 minutes
Servings: 42
Ingredients:

- 1 cup bread crumbs, seasoned
- 1 small chopped onion
- 1 large lightly beaten egg
- 3 minced garlic cloves
- 1 teaspoon salt
- 1/2 teaspoon pepper
- 16-ounce 90% lean ground beef
- 16-ounce ground pork

Sauce:

- 1-21 ounce can cherry pie filling
- 1/3 cup sherry (or substitute chicken broth)
- 1/3 cup of cider vinegar
- 1/4 cup of steak sauce
- 2 tablespoons of brown sugar
- 2 tablespoons soy sauce, reduced-sodium
- 1 teaspoon honey

Directions:

1. Preheat your oven to 400°F.

2. Mix the first six fixings and mix well. Add the ground meat and mix thoroughly. Shape the mixture into 1-inch balls. Arrange in a shallow baking pan over a greased rack.
3. Bake for 11 to 13 minutes or until cooked through. Drain juice on a paper towel.
4. In a large-size saucepan, combine all sauce ingredients. Boil the sauce over medium heat. Simmer uncovered within 2 to 3 minutes or until it thickens.
5. Add the meatballs stir gently until heated through.

Nutrition:

- Calories: 76
- Carbohydrates: 7g
- Fiber: 0g
- Fats: 3g
- Sodium: 169 mg
- Protein: 5g

Chapter 6. Bread & Pizza

67. Fig Relish Panini

Preparation Time: 15 minutes
Cooking Time: 30 minutes
Servings: 4
Ingredients:
- Grated parmesan cheese, for garnish
- Olive oil
- Arugula
- Basil leaves
- Toma cheese, grated or sliced
- Sweet butter
- 4 ciabatta slices

Fig Relish:
- 1 tsp dry mustard
- Pinch of salt
- 1 tsp mustard seed
- ½ cup apple cider vinegar
- ½ cup of sugar

- ½ lb. Mission figs stemmed and peeled

Directions:

1. Create fig relish by mincing the figs. Then put in all ingredients, except for the dry mustard, in a small pot and simmer for 30 minutes until it becomes jam-like.
2. Season with dry mustard according to taste and let cool before refrigerating.
3. Spread sweet butter on two slices of ciabatta rolls and layer on the following: cheese, basil leaves, arugula, and fig relish, then cover with the remaining bread slice.
4. Grill the Panini until cheese is melted and bread is crisped and ridged.

Nutrition:

- Calories: 264
- Carbs: 55.1g
- Protein: 6.0g
- Fat: 4.2g

68. Fruity and Cheesy Quesadilla

Preparation Time: 15 minutes
Cooking Time: 15 minutes
Servings: 1
Ingredients:

- ¼ cup hand-grated jack cheese
- ½ cup finely chopped fresh mango
- 1 large whole-grain tortilla
- 1 tbsp. chopped fresh cilantro

Directions:

1. In a medium bowl, mix cilantro and mango.
2. Place mango mixture inside tortilla and top with cheese.
3. Pop in a preheated 350°F oven and bake until cheese is melted entirely, around 10 to 15 minutes.

Nutrition:

- Calories: 169

- Fat: 9g
- Protein: 7g
- Carbohydrates: 15g

69. Garlic & Tomato Gluten Free Focaccia

Preparation Time: 15 minutes
Cooking Time: 20 minutes
Servings: 8
Ingredients:
- 1 egg
- ½ tsp lemon juice
- 1 tbsp. honey
- 4 tbsp. olive oil
- A pinch of sugar
- 1 ¼ cup warm water
- 1 tbsp. active dry yeast
- 2 tsp rosemary, chopped
- 2 tsp thyme, chopped
- 2 tsp basil, chopped
- 2 cloves garlic, minced
- 1 ¼ tsp sea salt
- 2 tsp xanthan gum
- ½ cup millet flour
- 1 cup potato starch, not flour
- 1 cup sorghum flour
- Gluten-free cornmeal for dusting

Directions:
1. For 5 minutes, turn on the oven and then turn it off while keeping the oven door closed.
2. In a small bowl, mix warm water and a pinch of sugar. Add yeast and swirl gently. Leave for 7 minutes.
3. In a large mixing bowl, whisk well herbs, garlic, salt, xanthan gum, starch, and flours.

4. Once the yeast is done proofing, pour into a bowl of flour. Whisk in egg, lemon juice, honey, and olive oil. Mix thoroughly and place in a well-greased square pan, dusted with cornmeal.
5. Top with fresh garlic, more herbs, and sliced tomatoes. Place in the warmed oven and let it rise for half an hour.
6. Turn on the oven to 375°F, and after preheating, set it for 20 minutes. Focaccia is done once tops are lightly browned.
7. Remove from the oven and pan immediately and let it cool. Best served when warm.

Nutrition:

- Calories: 251
- Carbs: 38.4g
- Protein: 5.4g
- Fat: 9.0g

70. Garlic-Rosemary Dinner Rolls

Preparation Time: 15 minutes
Cooking Time: 20 minutes
Servings: 8
Ingredients:
- 2garlic cloves, minced
- 1 tsp dried crushed rosemary
- ½ tsp apple cider vinegar
- 2 tbsp. olive oil
- 2 eggs
- 1 ¼ tsp salt
- 1 ¾ tsp xanthan gum
- ½ cup tapioca starch
- ¾ cup brown rice flour
- 1 cup sorghum flour
- 2 tsp dry active yeast
- 1 tbsp. honey
- ¾ cup hot water

Directions:

1. Mix well water and honey in a small bowl and add yeast. Leave it for exactly 7 minutes.
2. In a large bowl, mix the following with a paddle mixer: garlic, rosemary, salt, xanthan gum, sorghum flour, tapioca starch, and brown rice flour.
3. In a medium bowl, whisk vinegar, olive oil, and eggs.
4. Into the bowl of dry fixings, pour in vinegar and yeast mixture, and mix well.
5. Grease a 12-muffin tin with cooking spray. Transfer dough evenly into 12 muffin tins and leave it 20 minutes to rise.
6. Then preheat oven to 375°F and bake dinner rolls until tops are golden brown, around 17 to 19 minutes.
7. Remove dinner rolls from the oven and muffin tins immediately and let them cool. Best served when warm.

Nutrition:

- Calories: 200
- Carbs: 34.3g
- Protein: 4.2g
- Fat: 5.4g

71. Grilled Burgers with Mushrooms

Preparation Time: 15 minutes
Cooking Time: 10 minutes
Servings: 4
Ingredients:

- 2 Bibb lettuce, halved
- 4 slices red onion
- 4 slices tomato
- 4 whole wheat buns, toasted
- 2 tbsp. olive oil
- ¼ tsp cayenne pepper, optional
- 1garlic clove, minced
- 1 tbsp. sugar
- ½ cup of water

- 1/3 cup balsamic vinegar
- 4 large Portobello mushroom caps, around 5-inches in diameter

Directions:
1. Remove stems from mushrooms and clean with a damp cloth. Transfer into a baking dish with gill-side up.
2. In a bowl, mix thoroughly olive oil, cayenne pepper, garlic, sugar, water, and vinegar. Pour over mushrooms and marinate mushrooms in the ref for at least an hour.
3. Once the one hour is nearly up, preheat grill to medium-high fire and grease grill grate.
4. Grill mushrooms for five minutes per side or until tender. Baste mushrooms with the marinade, so it doesn't dry up.
5. To assemble, place ½ of the bread bun on a plate, top with a slice of onion, mushroom, tomato, and one lettuce leaf.
6. Cover with the other top half of the bun. Repeat the process with the remaining ingredients, serve, and enjoy.

Nutrition:

- Calories: 244.1
- Carbs: 32g
- Protein: 8.1g
- Fat: 9.3g

72. Herbed Panini Fillet O'Fish

Preparation Time: 15 minutes
Cooking Time: 25 minutes
Servings: 4
Ingredients:
- 4 slices thick sourdough bread
- 4 slices mozzarella cheese
- 1 portabella mushroom, sliced
- 1 small onion, sliced
- 6 tbsp. oil
- 4garlic and herb fish fillets

Directions:

1. Prepare your fillets by adding salt, pepper, and herbs (rosemary, thyme, parsley, whatever you like).
2. Then mix in the flour before deep frying in boiling oil. Once nicely browned, remove from oil and set aside.
3. On medium-high fire, sauté for five minutes the onions and mushroom in a skillet with 2 tbsp. oil.
4. Prepare sourdough bread by layering the following: cheese, fish fillet, onion mixture, and cheese again before covering with another bread slice.
5. Grill in your Panini press until cheese is melted and bread is crisped and ridged.

Nutrition:

- Calories: 422
- Carbs: 13.2g
- Protein: 51.2g
- Fat: 17.2g

73. Italian Flat Bread Gluten-Free

Preparation Time: 15 minutes
Cooking Time: 30 minutes
Servings: 8
Ingredients:

- 1 tbsp. apple cider
- 2 tbsp. water
- ½ cup yogurt
- 2 tbsp. butter
- 2 tbsp. sugar
- 2 eggs
- 1 tsp xanthan gum
- ½ tsp salt
- 1 tsp baking soda
- 1 ½ tsp baking powder
- ½ cup potato starch, not potato flour
- ½ cup tapioca flour

- ¼ cup brown rice flour
- 1/3 cup sorghum flour

Directions:
1. With parchment paper, line an 8 x 8-inch baking pan and grease parchment paper. Preheat oven to 375°F.
2. Mix xanthan gum, salt, baking soda, baking powder, all flours, and starch in a large bowl.
3. Whisk well sugar and eggs in a medium bowl until creamed. Add vinegar, water, yogurt, and butter. Whisk thoroughly.
4. Pour in the egg mixture into a bowl of flour and mix well. Transfer sticky dough into prepared pan and bake in the oven for 25 to 30 minutes.
5. If the tops of bread start to brown a lot, cover the top with foil and continue baking until done.
6. Remove from the oven and pan right away and let it cool. Best served when warm.

Nutrition:

- Calories: 166
- Carbs: 27.8g
- Protein: 3.4g
- Fat: 4.8g

74. Breakfast Pizza

Preparation Time: 15 minutes
Cooking Time: 30 minutes
Servings: 6
Ingredients:
- 2 tablespoons coconut flour
- 2 cups cauliflower, grated
- ½ teaspoon salt
- 1 tablespoon psyllium husk powder
- 4 eggs

Toppings:
- Avocado

- Smoked Salmon
- Herbs
- Olive oil
- Spinach

Directions:
1. Warm the oven to 360 degrees, then grease a pizza tray.
2. Mix all ingredients in a bowl, except toppings, and keep aside.
3. Pour the pizza dough onto the pan and mold it into an even pizza crust using hands.
4. Top the pizza with toppings and transfer to the oven.
5. Bake within 15 minutes until golden brown and remove from the oven to serve.

Nutrition:

- Calories: 454
- Carbs: 16g
- Fats: 31g
- Proteins: 22g
- Sodium: 1325mg
- Sugar: 4.4g

75. Coconut Flour Pizza

Preparation Time: 15 minutes
Cooking Time: 35 minutes
Servings: 4
Ingredients:
- 2 tablespoons psyllium husk powder
- ¾ cup coconut flour
- 1 teaspoon garlic powder
- ½ teaspoon salt
- ½ teaspoon baking soda
- 1 cup boiling water
- 1 teaspoon apple cider vinegar
- 3 eggs

Toppings:
- 3 tablespoons tomato sauce
- 1½ oz. Mozzarella cheese
- 1 tablespoon basil, freshly chopped

Directions:
1. Warm-up the oven to 350 degrees F, then oil a baking sheet.
2. Mix coconut flour, salt, psyllium husk powder, and garlic powder until thoroughly combined. Add eggs, apple cider vinegar, and baking soda and knead with boiling water.
3. Place the dough out on a baking sheet and top with the toppings—Bake within 20 minutes. Dish out and serve warm.

Nutrition:

- Calories: 173
- Carbs: 16.8g
- Fats: 7.4g
- Proteins: 10.4g
- Sodium: 622mg
- Sugar: 0.9g

76. Mini Pizza Crusts

Preparation Time: 15 minutes
Cooking Time: 20 minutes
Servings: 4
Ingredients:
- 1 cup coconut flour, sifted
- 8 large eggs, 5 whole eggs, and 3 egg whites
- ½ teaspoon baking powder
- Italian spices, to taste
- Salt and black pepper, to taste

For the pizza sauce:
- 2garlic cloves, crushed
- 1 teaspoon dried basil
- ½ cup tomato sauce
- ¼ teaspoon of sea salt

Directions:
1. Warm the oven to 350 degrees F, then oiled a baking tray.
2. Mix eggs plus egg whites in a large bowl. Stir in the coconut flour, baking powder, Italian spices, salt, and black pepper.
3. Make small dough balls from this mixture and press them on the baking tray.
4. Transfer to the oven and bake for about 20 minutes. Allow pizza bases to cool and keep aside.
5. Combine all ingredients for the pizza sauce and sit at room temperature for half an hour.
6. Spread this pizza sauce over the pizza crusts and serve.

Nutrition:

- Calories: 170
- Carbs: 5.7g
- Fats: 10.5g
- Proteins: 13.6g
- Sodium: 461mg
- Sugar: 2.3g

77. Pepperoni Pizza

Preparation Time: 15 minutes
Cooking Time: 40 minutes
Servings: 4
Ingredients:
- Crust
- 6 oz. mozzarella cheese, shredded
- 4 eggs

Topping:
- 1 teaspoon dried oregano
- 1½ oz. pepperoni
- 3 tablespoons tomato paste
- 5 oz. mozzarella cheese, shredded
- Olives

Directions:

1. Warm the oven to 400 degrees F and grease a baking sheet.
2. Whisk eggs and cheese in a bowl and spread on a baking sheet.
3. Transfer to the oven and bake for about 15 minutes until golden. Remove from the oven and allow it to cool.
4. Increase the oven temperature to 450 degrees F. Spread the tomato paste on the crust and top with oregano, pepperoni, cheese, and olives on top.
5. Bake again within 10 minutes and serve hot.

Nutrition:

- Calories: 356
- Carbs: 6.1g
- Fats: 23.8g
- Proteins: 30.6g
- Sodium: 790mg
- Sugar: 1.8g

78. Thin Crust Low Carb Pizza

Preparation Time: 15 minutes
Cooking Time: 25 minutes
Servings: 6
Ingredients:
- 2 tablespoons tomato sauce
- 1/8 teaspoon black pepper
- 1/8 teaspoon chili flakes
- 1-piece low-carb pita bread
- 2 ounces' low-moisture mozzarella cheese
- 1/8 teaspoon garlic powder

Toppings:
- Bacon
- Roasted red peppers
- Spinach
- Olives
- Pesto

- Artichokes
- Salami
- Pepperoni
- Roast beef
- Prosciutto
- Avocado
- Ham
- Chili paste
- Sriracha

Directions:
1. Warm the oven to 450 degrees F, then oiled a baking dish.
2. Mix tomato sauce, black pepper, chili flakes, and garlic powder in a bowl and keep aside.
3. Place the low-carb pita bread in the oven and bake for about 2 minutes. Remove from the oven and spread the tomato sauce on it.
4. Add mozzarella cheese and top with your favorite toppings. Bake again for 3 minutes and dish out.

Nutrition:

- Calories: 254
- Carbs: 12.9g
- Fats: 16g
- Proteins: 19.3g
- Sodium: 255mg
- Sugar: 2.8g

79. BBQ Chicken Pizza

Preparation Time: 15 minutes
Cooking Time: 30 minutes
Servings: 4
Ingredients:
- Dairy-Free Pizza Crust
- 6 tablespoons Parmesan cheese

- 6 large eggs
- 3 tablespoons psyllium husk powder
- Salt and black pepper, to taste
- 1½ teaspoons Italian seasoning

Toppings:
- 6 oz. rotisserie chicken, shredded
- 4 oz. cheddar cheese
- 1 tablespoon mayonnaise
- 4 tablespoons tomato sauce
- 4 tablespoons BBQ sauce

Directions:
1. Warm the oven to 400 degrees F and grease a baking dish.
2. Place all Pizza Crust ingredients in an immersion blender and blend until smooth. Spread dough mixture onto the baking dish and transfer it to the oven.
3. Bake for about 10 minutes and top with favorite toppings. Bake for about 3 minutes and dish out.

Nutrition:

- Calories: 356
- Carbs: 2.9g
- Fats: 24.5g
- Proteins: 24.5g
- Sodium: 396mg
- Sugar: 0.6g

80. Buffalo Chicken Crust Pizza

Preparation Time: 15 minutes
Cooking Time: 25 minutes
Servings: 6
Ingredients:
- 1 cup whole milk mozzarella, shredded
- 1 teaspoon dried oregano
- 2 tablespoons butter

- 1-pound chicken thighs, boneless and skinless
- 1 large egg
- ¼ teaspoon black pepper
- ¼ teaspoon salt
- 1 stalk celery
- 3 tablespoons Franks Red Hot Original
- 1 stalk green onion
- 1 tablespoon sour cream
- 1-ounce bleu cheese, crumbled

Directions:

1. Warm the oven to 400 degrees F and grease a baking dish.
2. Process chicken thighs in a food processor until smooth. Transfer to a large bowl and add egg, ½ cup of shredded mozzarella, oregano, black pepper, and salt to form a dough.
3. Spread the chicken dough in the baking dish and transfer it to the oven. Bake for about 25 minutes and keep aside.
4. Meanwhile, heat butter and add celery, and cook for about 4 minutes—Mix Franks Red Hot Original with the sour cream in a small bowl.
5. Spread the sauce mixture over the crust, layer with the cooked celery and remaining ½ cup of mozzarella and the bleu cheese. Bake again within 10 minutes, until the cheese is melted.

Nutrition:

- Calories: 172
- Carbs: 1g
- Fats: 12.9g
- Proteins: 13.8g
- Sodium: 172mg
- Sugar: 0.2g

81. Fresh Bell Pepper Basil Pizza

Preparation Time: 15 minutes
Cooking Time: 25 minutes
Servings: 3
Ingredients:
Pizza Base:

- ½ cup almond flour
- 2 tablespoons cream cheese
- 1 teaspoon Italian seasoning
- ½ teaspoon black pepper
- 6 ounces' mozzarella cheese
- 2 tablespoons psyllium husk
- 2 tablespoons fresh Parmesan cheese
- 1 large egg
- ½ teaspoon salt

Toppings:

- 4 ounces' cheddar cheese, shredded
- ¼ cup Marinara sauce
- 2/3 medium bell pepper
- 1 medium vine tomato
- 3 tablespoons basil, fresh chopped

Directions:

1. Warm the oven to 400 degrees F and grease a baking dish.
2. Microwave mozzarella cheese for about 30 seconds and top with the remaining pizza crust.
3. Add the remaining pizza ingredients to the cheese and mix. Flatten the dough and transfer it to the oven.
4. Bake for about 10 minutes. Remove, and top the pizza with the toppings and bake for another 10 minutes. Remove pizza from the oven and allow it to cool.

Nutrition:

- Calories: 411
- Carbs: 6.4g
- Fats: 31.3g
- Proteins: 22.2g; Sodium: 152mg; Sugar: 2.8g

Chapter 7. Fruits and Dessert Recipes

82. Chocolate Ganache

Preparation Time: 10 minutes
Cooking Time: 16 minutes
Servings: 16
Ingredients:
- 9 ounces' bittersweet chocolate, chopped
- 1 cup heavy cream
- 1 tablespoon dark rum (optional)

Directions:
1. Situate chocolate in a medium bowl. Cook cream in a small saucepan over medium heat.
2. Bring to a boil. When the cream has reached a boiling point, pour the chopped chocolate over it and beat until smooth. Stir the rum if desired.
3. Allow the ganache to cool slightly before you pour it on a cake. Begin in the middle of the cake and work outside. For a fluffy icing or chocolate filling, let it cool until thick and beat with a whisk until light and fluffy.

Nutrition:

- Calories: 142
- Fat: 10.8g
- Protein: 1.4g

83. Chocolate Covered Strawberries

Preparation Time: 15 minutes
Cooking Time: 0 minute
Servings: 24
Ingredients:
- 16 ounces' milk chocolate chips

- 2 tablespoons shortening
- 1-pound fresh strawberries with leaves

Directions:
1. In a bain-marie, melt chocolate and shortening, occasionally stirring until smooth. Pierce the tops of the strawberries with toothpicks and immerse them in the chocolate mixture.
2. Turn the strawberries and put the toothpick in Styrofoam so that the chocolate cools.

Nutrition:

- Calories: 115
- Fat: 7.3g
- Protein: 1.4g

84. Strawberry Angel Food Dessert

Preparation Time: 15 minutes
Cooking Time: 0 minutes
Servings: 18
Ingredients:
- 1 angel cake (10 inches)
- 2 packages of softened cream cheese
- 1 cup of white sugar
- 1 container (8 oz.) of frozen fluff, thawed
- 1 liter of fresh strawberries, sliced
- 1 jar of strawberry icing

Directions:
1. Crumble the cake in a 9 x 13-inch dish.
2. Beat the cream cheese and sugar in a medium bowl until the mixture is light and fluffy. Stir in the whipped topping. Crush the cake with your hands, and spread the cream cheese mixture over the cake.
3. Combine the strawberries and the frosting in a bowl until the strawberries are well covered. Spread over the layer of cream cheese. Cool until ready to serve.

Nutrition:

- Calories: 261
- Fat: 11g
- Protein: 3.2g

85. Fruit Pizza

Preparation Time: 30 minutes
Cooking Time: 0 minute
Servings: 8
Ingredients:
- 1 (18-oz) package sugar cookie dough
- 1 (8-oz) package cream cheese, softened
- 1 (8-oz) frozen filling, defrosted
- 2 cups of freshly cut strawberries
- 1/2 cup of white sugar
- 1 pinch of salt
- 1 tablespoon corn flour
- 2 tablespoons lemon juice
- 1/2 cup orange juice
- 1/4 cup water
- 1/2 teaspoon orange zest

Directions:
1. Ready oven to 175°C Slice the cookie dough then places it on a greased pizza pan. Press the dough flat into the mold. Bake for 10 to 12 minutes. Let cool.
2. Soften the cream cheese in a large bowl and then stir in the whipped topping. Spread over the cooled crust.
3. Start with strawberries cut in half. Situate in a circle around the outer edge. Continue with the fruit of your choice by going to the center. If you use bananas, immerse them in lemon juice. Then make a sauce with a spoon on the fruit.
4. Combine sugar, salt, corn flour, orange juice, lemon juice, and water in a pan. Boil and stir over medium heat. Boil for 1 or 2 minutes until thick. Remove from heat and add the grated orange zest. Place on the fruit.
5. Allow to cool for two hours, cut into quarters, and serve.

Nutrition:

- Calories: 535
- Fat: 30g
- Protein: 5.5g

86. Rhubarb Strawberry Crunch

Preparation Time: 15 minutes
Cooking Time: 45 minutes
Servings: 18
Ingredients:
- 1 cup of white sugar
- 3 tablespoons all-purpose flour
- 3 cups of fresh strawberries, sliced
- 3 cups of rhubarb, cut into cubes
- 1 1/2 cup flour
- 1 cup packed brown sugar
- 1 cup butter
- 1 cup oatmeal

Directions:
1. Preheat the oven to 190°C.
2. Combine white sugar, 3 tablespoons flour, strawberries, and rhubarb in a large bowl. Place the mixture in a 9 x 13-inch baking dish.
3. Mix 1 1/2 cups of flour, brown sugar, butter, and oats until a crumbly texture is obtained. You may want to use a blender for this. Crumble the mixture of rhubarb and strawberry.
4. Bake for 45 minutes.

Nutrition:

- Calories: 253
- Fat: 10.8g
- Protein: 2.3g

87. Chocolate Chip Banana Dessert

Preparation Time: 20 minutes
Cooking Time: 20 minutes
Servings: 24
Ingredients:
- 2/3 cup white sugar
- 3/4 cup butter
- 2/3 cup brown sugar
- 1 egg, beaten slightly
- 1 teaspoon vanilla extract
- 1 cup of banana puree
- 1 3/4 cup flour
- 2 teaspoons baking powder
- 1/2 teaspoon of salt
- 1 cup of semi-sweet chocolate chips

Directions:
1. Ready the oven to 175°C Grease and bake a 10 x 15-inch baking pan.
2. Beat the butter, white sugar, and brown sugar in a large bowl until light. Beat the egg and vanilla. Fold in the banana puree: mix baking powder, flour, and salt in another bowl. Mix flour mixture into the butter mixture. Stir in the chocolate chips. Spread in pan.
3. Bake for 20 minutes. Cool before cutting into squares.

Nutrition:

- Calories: 174
- Fat: 8.2g
- Protein: 1.7g

88. Apple Pie Filling

Preparation Time: 20 minutes
Cooking Time: 12 minutes
Servings: 40
Ingredients:

- 18 cups chopped apples
- 3 tablespoons lemon juice
- 10 cups of water
- 4 1/2 cups of white sugar
- 1 cup corn flour
- 2 teaspoons of ground cinnamon
- 1 teaspoon of salt
- 1/4 teaspoon ground nutmeg

Directions:

1. Mix apples with lemon juice in a large bowl and set aside. Pour the water into a Dutch oven over medium heat. Combine sugar, corn flour, cinnamon, salt, and nutmeg in a bowl. Add to water, mix well, and bring to a boil. Cook for 2 minutes with continuous stirring.
2. Boil apples again. Reduce the heat, cover, and simmer for 8 minutes. Allow cooling for 30 minutes.
3. Pour into five freezer containers and leave 1/2 inch of free space. Cool to room temperature.
4. Seal and freeze

Nutrition:

- Calories: 129
- Fat: 0.1g
- Protein: 0.2g

89. Ice Cream Sandwich Dessert

Preparation Time: 20 minutes
Cooking Time: 0 minute
Servings: 12
Ingredients:
- 22 ice cream sandwiches
- Frozen whipped topping in 16 oz. container, thawed
- 1 jar (12 oz.) Caramel ice cream
- 1 1/2 cups of salted peanuts

Directions:
1. Cut a sandwich with ice in two. Place a whole sandwich and a half sandwich on a short side of a 9 x 13-inch baking dish. Repeat this until the bottom is covered, alternate the full sandwich, and the half sandwich.
2. Spread half of the whipped topping. Pour the caramel over it. Sprinkle with half the peanuts. Do layers with the rest of the ice cream sandwiches, whipped cream, and peanuts.
3. Cover and freeze for up to 2 months. Remove from the freezer 20 minutes before serving. Cut into squares.

Nutrition:

- Calories: 559
- Fat: 28.8g
- Protein: 10g

90. Cranberry and Pistachio Biscotti

Preparation Time: 15 minutes
Cooking Time: 35 minutes
Servings: 36
Ingredients:
- 1/4 cup light olive oil
- 3/4 cup white sugar
- 2 teaspoons vanilla extract
- 1/2 teaspoon almond extract

- 2 eggs
- 1 3/4 cup all-purpose flour
- 1/4 teaspoon salt
- 1 teaspoon baking powder
- 1/2 cup dried cranberries
- 1 1/2 cup pistachio nuts

Directions:

1. Prep oven to 150°C.
2. Combine the oil and sugar in a large bowl until a homogeneous mixture is obtained. Stir in the vanilla and almond extract and add the eggs. Combine flour, salt, and baking powder; gradually add to the egg mixture—mix cranberries and nuts by hand.
3. Divide the dough in half—form two 12 x 2-inch logs on a parchment baking sheet. The dough can be sticky, wet hands with cold water to make it easier to handle the dough.
4. Bake in the preheated oven for 35 minutes or until the blocks are golden brown. Pullout from the oven and let cool for 10 minutes. Reduce oven heat to 275 degrees F (135 degrees C).
5. Cut diagonally into 3/4-inch-thick slices. Place on the sides on the baking sheet covered with parchment—Bake for about 8 to 10 minutes

Nutrition:

- Calories: 92
- Fat: 4.3g
- Protein: 2.1g

91. Cream Puff Dessert

Preparation Time: 20 minutes
Cooking Time: 36 minutes
Servings: 12
Ingredients:
Puff:

- 1 cup water
- 1/2 cup butter

- 1 cup all-purpose flour
- 4 eggs

Filling:
- 1 (8-oz) package cream cheese, softened
- 3 1/2 cups cold milk
- 2 (4-oz) packages instant chocolate pudding mix

Topping:
- 1 (8-oz) package frozen whipped cream topping, thawed
- 1/4 cup topping with milk chocolate flavor
- 1/4 cup caramel filling
- 1/3 cup almond flakes

Directions:
1. Set oven to 200 degrees C (400 degrees F). Grease a 9 x 13-inch baking dish.
2. Melt the butter in the water in a medium-sized pan over medium heat. Pour the flour in one go and mix vigorously until the mixture forms a ball. Remove from heat and let stand for 5 minutes. Beat the eggs one by one until they are smooth and shiny. Spread in the prepared pan.
3. Bake in the preheated oven for 30 to 35 minutes, until puffed and browned. Cool completely on a rack.
4. While the puff pastry cools, mix the cream cheese mixture, the milk, and the pudding. Spread over the cooled puff pastry. Cool for 20 minutes.
5. Spread whipped cream on cooled topping and sprinkle with chocolate and caramel sauce. Sprinkle with almonds. Freeze 1 hour before serving.

Nutrition:

- Calories: 355
- Fat: 22.3g
- Protein: 8.7g

92. Fresh Peach Dessert

Preparation Time: 30 minutes
Cooking Time: 27 minutes
Servings: 15
Ingredients:

- 16 whole graham crackers, crushed
- 3/4 cup melted butter
- 1/2 cup white sugar
- 4 1/2 cups of miniature marshmallows
- 1/4 cup of milk
- 1 pint of heavy cream
- 1/3 cup of white sugar
- 6 large fresh peaches—peeled, seeded, and sliced

Directions:

1. In a bowl, mix the crumbs from the graham cracker, melted butter, and 1/2 cup of sugar. Mix until a homogeneous mixture is obtained, save 1/4 cup of the mixture for filling. Squeeze the rest of the mixture into the bottom of a 9 x 13-inch baking dish.
2. Heat marshmallows and milk in a large pan over low heat and stir until marshmallows are completely melted. Remove from heat and let cool.
3. Beat the cream in a large bowl until soft peaks occur. Beat 1/3 cup of sugar until the cream forms firm spikes. Add the whipped cream to the cooled marshmallow mixture.
4. Divide half of the cream mixture over the crust, place the peaches over the cream and divide the rest of the cream mixture over the peaches. Sprinkle the crumb mixture on the cream. Cool until ready to serve.

Nutrition:

- Calories: 366
- Fat: 25.5g
- Protein: 1.9g

93. Blueberry Dessert

Preparation Time: 30 minutes
Cooking Time: 20 minutes
Servings: 28
Ingredients:

- 1/2 cup butter
- 2 cups white sugar
- 36graham crackers, crushed
- 4 eggs
- 2 packets of cream cheese, softened
- 1 teaspoon vanilla extract
- 2 cans of blueberry pie filling
- 1 package (16-oz) frozen whipped cream, thawed

Directions:

1. Cook butter and sprinkle 1 cup of sugar and graham crackers. Squeeze this mixture into a 9x13 dish.
2. Beat the eggs. Gradually beat the cream cheese, sugar, and vanilla in the eggs.
3. Pour the mixture of eggs and cream cheese over the graham cracker crust. Bake for 15 to 20 minutes at 165°C (325°F). Cool.
4. Pour the blueberry pie filling on top of the baked dessert. Spread non-dairy whipped topping on fruit. Cool until ready to serve.

Nutrition:

- Calories: 354
- Fat: 15.4g
- Protein: 3.8g

94. Good Sweet

Preparation Time: 10 minutes
Cooking Time: 10 minutes
Servings: 2
Ingredients:

- ¼ teaspoon tomatoes, chopped
- ¼ teaspoon cucumber, chopped
- 2 tablespoons honey
- Other veggies/beans optional

Directions:

1. Whisk the ingredients well.
2. In a bowl, toss to coat with honey as smoothly as possible.

Nutrition:

- Calories: 187
- Fat: 15.6g
- Protein: 2g

95. A Taste of Dessert

Preparation Time: 15 minutes
Cooking Time: 0 minutes
Servings: 2
Ingredients:

- 1 tablespoon cilantro
- 1 tablespoon green onion
- 1 peeled mango, seeded and chopped
- ¼ cup bell pepper, chopped
- 2 tablespoons honey

Directions:

1. Incorporate all the ingredients.
2. Serve when combined well.

Nutrition:

- Calories: 21
- Fat: 0.1g
- Protein: 0.3g

96. Honey Carrots

Preparation Time: 5 minutes
Cooking Time: 15 minutes
Servings: 2
Ingredients:
- 16 ounces baby carrots
- ¼ cup brown sugar

Directions:

1. Boil carrots with water in a huge pot
2. Drain after 15 minutes, and steam for 2 minutes.
3. Stir in the sugar, and serve when mixed well.

Nutrition:

- Calories: 402
- Fat: 23.3g
- Protein: 1.4g

97. Fresh Cherry Treat

Preparation Time: 10 minutes
Cooking Time: 10 minutes
Servings: 2
Ingredients:
- 1 tablespoon honey
- 1 tablespoon almonds, crushed
- 12 ounces cherries

Directions:

1. Preheat the oven to 350°F, and for 5 minutes, bake the cherries.
2. Coat them with honey, and serve with almonds on top.

Nutrition:

- Calories: 448
- Fat: 36.4g
- Protein: 3.5g

98. Milky Peachy Dessert

Preparation Time: 15 minutes
Cooking Time: 10 minutes
Servings: 2
Ingredients:
- 1 fresh peach, peeled and sliced
- 1 teaspoon brown sugar
- 1 tablespoon milk

Directions:

1. Prepare a baking dish with a layer of peaches and toss in the milk.
2. Top the peaches with sugar, and bake at 350F for 5 minutes.

Nutrition:

- Calories: 366
- Fat: 22.5g
- Protein: 1.9g

99. Citrus Sections

Preparation Time: 20 minutes
Cooking Time: 5 minutes
Servings: 2
Ingredients:
- 1grapefruit, peeled and sectioned
- ½ cup pineapple chunks
- 1 small orange, sectioned into chunks
- ½ tablespoon brown sugar
- ½ teaspoon butter, low fat and unsalted, melted

Directions:

- Preheat an oven tray at 350`F.
- Set the fruits on the tray, and top with the brown sugar, mixed with the butter, and bake for 5 minutes.
- Transfer to a platter.

Nutrition:

- Calories: 279
- Fat: 5.9g
- Protein: 2.2g

100.   After Meal Apples

Preparation Time: 15 minutes
Cooking Time: 25 minutes
Servings: 2
Ingredients:
- 1 whole apple, cut into chunks
- ½ cup pineapple chunks
- ½ cup grapes, seedless
- ¼ cup orange juice
- ¼ teaspoon cinnamon

Directions:

1. Preheat the oven to 350°F.
2. Add all the fruits to a baking dish.
3. Drizzle with the orange juice and sprinkle with cinnamon.
4. Bake for 25 minutes, and serve hot.

Nutrition:

- Calories: 124
- Fat: 3.2g
- Protein: 0.8g

101. Warm Nut Bites

Preparation Time: 10 minutes
Cooking Time: 20 minutes
Servings: 2
Ingredients:
- 4 tablespoons honey
- 2 cups almonds
- 1 tablespoon almond oil

Directions:

1. Layer the almonds, whole, on a baking sheet.
2. Bake for 15 minutes at 350°F.
3. Turn half way, and roll the almonds in honey.
4. Serve.

Nutrition:

- Calories: 268
- Fat: 19.7g
- Protein: 7.6g

102.   Dipped Sprouts

Preparation Time: 12 minutes
Cooking Time: 10 minutes
Servings: 2
Ingredients:

- 16 ounces brussels sprouts
- 4 tablespoons honey
- 6 tablespoons raisins and nuts, crushed

Directions:

1. Boil water in a pot.
2. Add sprouts, and cook for 10 minutes until soft.
3. Glaze the sprouts in honey, and coat well. Add nuts and raisins.

Nutrition:

- Calories: 221
- Fat: 15.1g
- Protein: 5.3g

103.   Pecans and Cheese

Preparation Time: 20 minutes
Cooking Time: 0 minutes
Servings: 2
Ingredients:

- 1 teaspoon cinnamon, ground
- 4 ounces feta cheese
- 2 ounces pecans, finely chopped
- 2 tablespoons honey
- 2 sprigs rosemary, fresh, minced

Directions:

1. Make small balls of cheese.

2. Crush the pecans and place them in a shallow bowl with the cinnamon.
3. Roll the cheese in the pecans and cinnamon.
4. Drizzle honey over the balls.
5. Serve with rosemary on top.

Nutrition:

- Calories: 234
- Fat: 18.6g
- Protein: 7.5g

Chapter 8. 14 Day Meal Day Plan

Day	Breakfast	Lunch	Dinner	Fruit/Desserts
1	Greek Style Frittata with Spinach and Feta Cheese	Salmon Stew	Pork in Blue Cheese Sauce	Chocolate Ganache
2	Cheese & Cauliflower Bake	Asparagus Salmon Fillets	Mississippi Pulled Pork	Chocolate Covered Strawberries
3	Ham & Cheese Broccoli Brunch Bowl	Crispy Baked Chicken	Spicy and Cheesy Turkey Dip	Strawberry Angel Food Dessert
4	Zucchini & Spinach with Bacon	Sour and Sweet Fish	Turkey Chorizo with Bok Choy	Fruit Pizza
5	Pepperoni Pizza with Meat Crust	Creamy Chicken	Spicy Chicken Breasts	Rhubarb Strawberry Crunch
6	The Better Quiche Lorraine	Paprika Butter Shrimp	Saucy Boston Butt	Chocolate Chip Banana Dessert
7	Spinach & Sausage Pizza	Almond Flour Burger with Goat Cheese	Old-Fashioned Goulash	Apple Pie Filling
8	Eggplant & Sausage Bake	Sausage Skillet with Cabbage	Flatbread with Chicken Liver Pâté	Ice Cream Sandwich Dessert
9	Three-Cheese Artichoke Hearts Bake	Chicken and Broccoli Gratin	Sunday Chicken with Cauliflower Salad	Cranberry and Pistachio Biscotti

10	Tomato Eggs	Chicken Curry	Authentic Turkey Kebabs	Cream Puff Dessert
11	Sun-Dried Tomatoes Salad	Bacon Wrapped Asparagus	Mexican-style Turkey Bacon Bites	Fresh Peach Dessert
12	Greek Bowl	Spinach Chicken	Easy Fall-Off-The-Bone Ribs	Blueberry Dessert
13	Morning Oats	Lemongrass Prawns	Brie-Stuffed Meatballs	Good Sweet
14	Yogurt with Dates	Stuffed Mushrooms	Roasted Leg Lamb	A Taste of Dessert

Conclusion

I would like to thank my readers for finishing the book and making it this far. I wish you the best of luck on your Ketogenic Mediterranean diet journey. I thought I would take a minute in the conclusion to just lay out a few general rules to follow the art of a Ketogenic Mediterranean diet. The first rule is that you can consume as many green vegetables as you want. So you can eat all the spinach, arugula, celery, Broccoli that you please. No matter what vegetables you consume, be sure to liberally drown them in olive oil. I whole heartily recommend that you consume nuts and avocados daily. However, both can be high in calories, and although we don't normally count calories or worry about portions on a keto diet, you should limit yourself to one handful of nuts per day, and one or two avocados per day. Other limitations you should keep in mind are that you only eat berries in moderate amounts. I would say a quarter cup per serving, and you can definitely eat tomatoes, but you should also limit those within reason. If you find that you're having trouble losing weight, you might want to take a look at your berry consumption. They are low-sugar fruits, but for some people, they can cause problems in the initial stages of the diet.

So now let's talk about meat consumption. My recommendation is to have one serving of fatty fish per day. That isn't necessarily palatable for everyone, but you should have fish at least five times a week if you're going to call it a Mediterranean diet. The other meals you're going to have can contain meat once or twice per day. You can vary your meats including poultry, pork, lamb, and of course beef. I really do not recommend eating low-fat cuts of meat even though the experts have been recommending that on a Mediterranean diet. Lean meats are fine if you're eating carbohydrates because the carbs are where your energy comes from. But if you have cut out whole grains, fruits, and potatoes, etc., you have to get your energy somewhere else. You can in part get it from all of the oil, and as we've emphasized over and over, you should consume as much olive oil as possible. However, when it gets down to it, you are going to need to eat some fatty meat in order to get adequate levels of energy. Also, remember that you can eat all the cheese that you want. You can have heavy cream and butter, but you should avoid milk, yogurt, and cottage cheese as these products contain too many carbohydrates.

And so we have come to the end of the book. I hope that it has been informative; and even if you don't strictly follow this kind of diet, I hope that it gives you some ideas of how to adjust whatever diet that you pursue. Thanks again for reading.

Printed in Great Britain
by Amazon